MW00577348

Thomas Goodwin

THOMAS GOODWIN (1600–1680)

(*A portrait by Joel Heflin, 2009*)

"A Habitual Sight of Him":

The Christ-Centered Piety of Thomas Goodwin

Introduced and Edited by
Joel R. Beeke and Mark Jones

Reformation Heritage Books
Grand Rapids, Michigan

"A Habitual Sight of Him"
© 2009 by Joel R. Beeke and Mark Jones

Published by
Reformation Heritage Books
2965 Leonard St., NE
Grand Rapids, MI 49525
616-977-0599 / Fax: 616-285-3246
e-mail: orders@heritagebooks.org
website: www.heritagebooks.org

Library of Congress Cataloging-in-Publication Data

Goodwin, Thomas, 1600-1680.
A habitual sight of Him : the Christ-centered piety of Thomas Goodwin / introduced and edited by Joel R. Beeke and Mark Jones.
p. cm. -- (Profiles in reformed spirituality)
Includes bibliographical references.
ISBN 978-1-60178-067-6 (pbk. : alk. paper)
1. Piety. 2. Spirituality. 3. Goodwin, Thomas, 1600-1680. I. Beeke, Joel R., 1952- II. Jones, Mark, 1980- III. Title.
BV4647.P5G66 2009
230'.59--dc22

2009028683

For additional Reformed literature, both new and used, request a free book list from Reformation Heritage Books at the above address.

With gratitude to

Adrian and Claire Slootmaker

models of Christ-centered piety; loyal,
God-fearing, enjoyable friends of three decades

I thank my God upon every
remembrance of you (Philippians 1:3).

— JRB

To my beloved friends at

Faith Vancouver PCA:

May these readings do for your souls
what they have done for my own,

that in all things he might have the
preeminence (Colossians 1:18).

—MJ

PROFILES IN REFORMED SPIRITUALITY
series editors—Joel R. Beeke and Michael A. G. Haykin

Other Books in the Series:

Michael Haykin, *"A Consuming Fire": The Piety of Alexander Whyte of Free St. George's*

Michael Haykin, *"A Sweet Flame": Piety in the Letters of Jonathan Edwards*

Michael Haykin and Steve Weaver, *"Devoted to the Service of the Temple": Piety, Persecution, and Ministry in the Writings of Hercules Collins*

Michael Haykin and Darrin R. Brooker, *"Christ Is All": The Piety of Horatius Bonar*

J. Stephen Yuille, *"Trading and Thriving in Godliness": The Piety of George Swinnock*

Joel R. Beeke, *"The Soul of Life": The Piety of John Calvin*

Thabiti Anyabwile, *"May We Meet in the Heavenly World": The Piety of Lemuel Haynes*

Table of Contents

Profiles in Reformed Spirituality xi
Acknowledgments xvii

Introduction: The Piety of
Thomas Goodwin (1600–1680) 1

1. Christ Excels Joseph 37
2. Christ Longs for His Own Return 41
3. Sitting in Heaven 45
4. Crying Us into Heaven 49
5. Christ's Gift 53
6. Christ Dwelling in Our Hearts by Faith. . . . 55
7. Christ's Perfections Are Our Perfections . . . 61
8. Three Hours 63
9. Christ by Piecemeal 65
10. Christ, the Marrow of the Gospel 67
11. Reconciliation Through Christ. 69
12. "Christ above Moses" 71
13. God's Greatest Work (1) 73
14. God's Greatest Work (2) 75
15. Possessing Christ by Faith 79
16. One Foot on Christ, Another on Yourself? . 81
17. No Union, No Justification 83
18. Communion with Christ 85
19. Elected to Inseparable Union with Christ . . 89
20. Purchasing and Bestowing. 91
21. Gathered to Christ or Satan? 93

22. Sitting at the Right Hand 95
23. Summed Up in Christ 97
24. Christ Putting Beauty on the Body 99
25. Living Like Christ 101
26. The Revenues of His Death 103
27. Joy in God's Glory. 107
28. Weak, but Accepted for Christ's Sake 109
29. Christ's Works of Glory 111
30. Restoring Beauty to His Bride 113
31. "The Son's Special Act" 115
32. Spirit-Christology 117
33. Never Leaving Christ Out 121
34. The Mystery of His Will in Christ 125
35. Treasures in Heaven. 129
Reading Goodwin 133

Profiles in Reformed Spirituality

Charles Dickens' famous line in *A Tale of Two Cities*—"it was the best of times, it was the worst of times"—seems well suited to western Evangelicalism since the 1960s. On the one hand, these decades have seen much for which to praise God and to rejoice. In His goodness and grace, for instance, Reformed truth is no longer a house under siege. Growing numbers identify themselves theologically with what we hold to be biblical truth, namely, Reformed theology and piety. And yet, as an increasing number of Reformed authors have noted, there are many sectors of the surrounding western Evangelicalism that are characterized by great shallowness and a trivialization of the weighty things of God. So much of Evangelical worship seems barren. And when it comes to spirituality, there is little evidence of the riches of our heritage as Reformed Evangelicals.

As it was at the time of the Reformation, when the watchword was *ad fontes*—"back to the sources"—so it is now: the way forward is backward. We need to go back to the spiritual heritage of Reformed Evangelicalism to find the pathway forward. We cannot live in the past; to attempt to do so would be antiquarianism. But our Reformed forebearers in the faith can teach us much about Christianity, its doctrines, its passions, and its fruit.

And they can serve as our role models. As R. C. Sproul has noted of such giants as Augustine, Martin Luther, John Calvin, and Jonathan Edwards: "These men all were conquered, overwhelmed, and spiritually intoxicated by their vision of the holiness of God. Their minds and imaginations were captured by the majesty of God the Father. Each of them possessed a profound affection for the sweetness and excellence of Christ. There was in each of them a singular and unswerving loyalty to Christ that spoke of a citizenship in heaven that was always more precious to them than the applause of men."[1]

To be sure, we would not dream of placing these men and their writings alongside the Word of God. John Jewel (1522–1571), the Anglican apologist, once stated: "What say we of the fathers, Augustine, Ambrose, Jerome, Cyprian?... They were learned men, and learned fathers; the instruments of the mercy of God, and vessels full of grace. We despise them not, we read them, we reverence them, and give thanks unto God for them. Yet...we may not make them the foundation and warrant of our conscience: we may not put our trust in them. Our trust is in the name of the Lord."[2]

Seeking then both to honor the past and yet not idolize it, we are issuing these books in the series Profiles in Reformed Spirituality. The design is to introduce the spirituality and piety of the Reformed

---

1. "An Invaluable Heritage," *Tabletalk*, 23, no. 10 (October 1999): 5–6.

2. Cited in Barrington R. White, "Why Bother with History?" *Baptist History and Heritage*, 4, no. 2 (July 1969): 85.

tradition by presenting descriptions of the lives of notable Christians with select passages from their works. This combination of biographical sketches and collected portions from primary sources gives a taste of the subjects' contributions to our spiritual heritage and some direction as to how the reader can find further edification through their works. It is the hope of the publishers that this series will provide riches for those areas where we are poor and light of day where we are stumbling in the deepening twilight.

—Joel R. Beeke
Michael A. G. Haykin

Acknowledgments

Thirty-six selections of Thomas Goodwin's Christ-centered writings that promote piety are presented here in purist form. Only the smallest of changes have been made for consistency's sake, such as capitalization of a few words and the writing out in full of Bible books when not in parentheses. On a few occasions, lengthy paragraphs have been broken up into smaller paragraphs for the sake of readability. On rare occasions, a few words have been added in brackets to supply clarity. For the rest, the selections are precisely what are found in Goodwin's *Works*.

We owe thanks to Greg Bailey and Martha Fisher for editing this book; to Michael Haykin, co-editor of the series, for proofreading the work; to Derek Naves for hunting down illustrations; to Jay T. Collier for seeing this book through the press; and to Gary and Linda den Hollander, our effective proofing/typesetting team, for doing their normal high-quality work.

* * * * *

Most of all, I owe heartfelt thanks to my special wife, Mary, for her patience and love in supporting my writing ministry. No man could have a better helpmeet than the one with whom God has graciously chosen to bless me; daily, I thank the Lord for her. I also thank my children, Calvin, Esther, and Lydia. Without their great attitude and cooperation, I could never be involved in writing and editing.

Finally, I am so grateful for Thomas Goodwin, who, for more than a decade, has been my favorite Puritan to read. His profound way of experientially probing the depths of our depravity, then exalting the suitability, beauty, and glory of Christ in His mediatorial work, is unsurpassed. What a gift the church has in Goodwin! Read him for your soul's profit here, then buy his *Works* (www.heritagebooks.com) and read on for years. You won't be sorry.

—JRB

* * * * *

I owe thanks to my wife, Barb, who has been incredibly patient with me, especially during evenings as I've returned to the computer to finish up a number of projects such as this one. I am also grateful to my Ph.D. supervisor, Dr. Michael Haykin, who put my name forward for this small book. Finally, I, too, am grateful for Thomas Goodwin; his writings have been a constant companion of mine over the past two years. And because Christ figures so centrally in his *Works*, I have been blessed to read frequently of the one who is "chief among ten thousand."

—MJ

The Indwelling of Christ by faith...is to have Jesus Christ continually in one's eye, a habitual sight of Him. I call it so because a man actually does not always think of Christ; but as a man does not look up to the sun continually, yet he sees the light of it.... So you should carry along and bear along in your eye the sight and knowledge of Christ, so that at least a presence of Him accompanies you, which faith makes.

—Thomas Goodwin,
Works, 2:411

Thomas Goodwin

The Piety of Thomas Goodwin (1600–1680)

Considering Thomas Goodwin's theological and political influence in seventeenth-century England, it is remarkable that he is little known today, even within conservative Reformed evangelical circles. The reasons for Goodwin's relative obscurity today are several. For example, Goodwin was a Puritan and champion of ecclesiastical Independency (i.e. Congregationalism). Therefore, as a result of the political and religious upheaval in England during the 1640s and 1650s, culminating in the Great Ejection of 1662, Goodwin found himself on the "losing side." And, as Carl Trueman has noted, "non-conformists were not simply expelled from the Church of England, but excluded from the establishment, political, cultural, and intellectual, with all of the later impotence with regard to influence and the writing of history which that implies."[1] Furthermore, in connection to the Great Ejection, the paucity of secondary literature on Goodwin can be explained in part because of the Anglican monopoly of higher education that has continued into the twentieth century. The Puritans, especially Goodwin, "suffered the neglect which their separation from the Church

1. Carl Trueman, *John Owen* (Farnham, U.K.: Ashgate, 2007), 1.

made inevitable."[2] The legacy of Goodwin—or lack thereof—is not, then, the result of any intrinsic mediocrity in his thought, but rather the result of disadvantageous historical circumstances that relegated one of England's finest theologians to the halls of obscurity. Those, however, who have read Goodwin are capacious in their praise!

Renowned for intelligent piety at its Puritan best, Goodwin, known as "the Atlas of Independency," stands on a par with John Owen, "the prince of Puritans," as a theologian and an exegete, and often surpasses him in experimental depth. Any lover of the biblical and experimental emphases of the Puritans will find Goodwin both readable and spiritually rewarding. He represents the cream of Puritanism, capturing the intellect, will, and heart of his readers. His collected *Works* join the vigor of earlier Puritans such as William Perkins and Richard Sibbes to the matured thought of later Puritan divines, represented supremely by Owen.

Those influenced by Goodwin's writings include John Cotton, Jonathan Edwards, George Whitefield, and John Gill. Alexander Whyte confessed: "I have read no other author so much and so often. And I continue to read him to this day, as if I had never read him before." He calls Goodwin's sermon, "Christ Dwelling in Our Hearts by Faith," one of the "two very greatest sermons in the English language." Whyte aptly concludes:

> Goodwin is always an interpreter, and one of a

---

2. Carl Trueman, *Claims of Truth* (Carlisle, U.K.: Paternoster, 1998), 2.

thousand.... All his work, throughout his twelve volumes, is just so much pulpit exposition and pulpit application of the Word of God.... Full as Goodwin always is of the ripest scriptural and Reformation scholarship; full as he always is of the best theological and philosophical learning of his own day and of all foregoing days; full, also, as he always is of the deepest spiritual experience—all the same, he is always so simple, so clear, so direct, so un-technical, so personal, and so pastoral.[3]

In our generation, Puritan scholar J. I. Packer concurs: "Whyte called Goodwin 'the greatest pulpit exegete of Paul that has ever lived,' and perhaps justly; Goodwin's Biblical expositions are quite unique, even among the Puritans, in the degree to which they combine theological breadth with experimental depth. John Owen saw into the mind of Paul as clearly as Goodwin—sometimes, on points of detail, more clearly—but not even Owen ever saw so deep into Paul's heart."[4]

---

3. Alexander Whyte, *Thirteen Appreciations* (London: Oliphant, Anderson and Ferrier, 1913), 158ff.

4. J. I. Packer, "The Witness of the Spirit: The Puritan Teaching," in *The Wisdom of Our Fathers* (London: Puritan Conference, 1956), 14; cf. J. C. Philpot, *Reviews by the late Mr. J. C. Philpot* (London: Frederick Kirby, 1901), 2:479ff., who comments, "Being a man of choice experience, Goodwin so blends with [his sound expositions of doctrine] the work of the Spirit, in all its various branches, as to enrich his exposition with a heavenly savour and unction which carries with it great force, and commends itself in a very sensible and profitable manner to the conscience."

Education and Conversion

Thomas Goodwin was born on October 5, 1600, in Rollesby, Norfolk, to Richard (*d.* 1632) and Katherine Goodwin (1577–1645).[5] Richard was a churchwarden of St. Nicholas from 1615, who, in 1627, was reprimanded by Samuel Harsnett, bishop of Norwich, for allowing nonconformists to preach without the surplice. His parents' nonconformist sympathies

---

5. For biographical material on Goodwin, see *The Works of Thomas Goodwin,* 5 vols. (London: J. D. and S. R., 1704), 1:v–xix, by Thomas Goodwin Jr. (hereafter, "Life"); *The Works of Thomas Goodwin,* 12 vols. (Grand Rapids: Reformation Heritage Books, 2006), 1:1–23 by Joel R. Beeke (from which much of this introduction is drawn) and 2:ix–xlviii, by Robert Halley (hereafter, Halley, "Memoir"); Edmund Calamy, *The Nonconformist's Memorial,* ed. Samuel Palmer (London: Alex. Hogg, 1778), 1:183–87; James Reid, "Life of Thomas Goodwin," in *Memoirs of the Westminster Divines* (1811; reprint Edinburgh: Banner of Truth Trust, 1982), 319–43; Sir Leslie Stephen and Sir Sidney Lee, eds., *The Dictionary of National Biography* [DNB] (1890; reprint Oxford: Oxford University Press, 1922), 22:148–50; Whyte, *Thirteen Appreciations,* 157–76; Stanley P. Fienberg, "Thomas Goodwin, Puritan Pastor and Independent Divine" (Ph.D. dissertation, University of Chicago, 1974); Brian Freer, "Thomas Goodwin, the Peaceable Puritan," and Graham Harrison, "Thomas Goodwin and Independency," in *Diversities of Gifts,* Westminster Conference Reports, 1980 (London: The Westminster Conference, 1981), 7–44; Tom Webster, *Godly Clergy in Early Stuart England: The Caroline Puritan Movement, c. 1620–1643* (Cambridge: Cambridge University Press, 1997), 149–338; Michael Horton, "Thomas Goodwin and the Puritan Doctrine of Assurance: Continuity and Discontinuity in the Reformed Tradition, 1600–1680" (Ph.D. dissertation, University of Coventry and Wycliffe Hall, Oxford, 1998); T. M. Lawrence, "Transmission and transformation" (Ph.D. dissertation, Cambridge University, 2002); T. M. Lawrence, "Goodwin, Thomas (1600–1680)," *Oxford Dictionary of National Biography,* ed. H. C. G. Matthew and Brian Harrison (Oxford: Oxford University Press, 2004; online edn., 2008), 22:823–28.

St. Nicholas Parish Church,
where Goodwin's father was churchwarden
(*Photo courtesy of Paul Davies*)

geared Goodwin's education toward ecclesiastical involvement. On August 25, 1613, Goodwin entered Christ's College, Cambridge, which at that time was a "nest of Puritans."[6] At this time, the legacies of William Perkins (1558–1602) and William Ames (1576–1633) were "still fresh in most Men's Memories."[7] Upon his arrival at Christ's College, "there remain'd still in the College six Fellows that were

---

6. Benjamin Brook, *The Lives of the Puritans: Containing a Biographical Account of Those Divines Who Distinguished Themselves in the Cause of Religious Liberty, from the Reformation Under Queen Elizabeth, to the Act of Uniformity in 1662* (London: for J. Black, 1813), 113.

7. "Life," ix. Patrick Collinson argues that Perkins was "the prince of puritan theologians and the most eagerly read" (*The Elizabethan Puritan Movement* [Berkeley: University of California Press, 1967], 125). For a good discussion of Ames and Perkins's influence at Cambridge, see Paul R. Schaeffer Jr., "The Spiritual Brotherhood on the Habits of the Heart: Cambridge Protestants and the Doctrine

great Tutors, who professed Religion after the strictest sort, then called Puritans."[8] At Cambridge, Goodwin would have had a thorough training in humanism and scholasticism; logic, rhetoric, metaphysics, mathematics, physics, and linguistics formed the substance of his undergraduate curriculum.[9]

At Cambridge, Goodwin became acquainted with Zacharias Ursinus's (1534–1583) *Heidelberg Catechism* and followed the Arminian–Calvinist debates at Dort closely. Goodwin "judged [the Calvinists] to be in the right...and the Arminians in the wrong."[10] Moreover, as a student of theology, Goodwin came under the "plain and wholesome" preaching of Richard Sibbes (1577–1635) at Holy Trinity, Cambridge. Sibbes's preaching and the reading of John Calvin's *Institutes of the Christian Religion* were decisive in both the spiritual and theological formation of Goodwin. Speaking of Calvin's *Institutes,* Goodwin writes: "O how sweet was the reading of some Parts of that Book to me! How pleasing was the Delivery of Truths in a solid manner then to me!"[11]

In their preaching, Sibbes and John Preston (1587–1628) sought, according to Paul Schaeffer Jr., "a revitalization and reformation of piety in the lives of

---

of Sanctification from William Perkins to Thomas Shepard" (Ph.D. dissertation, Oxford University, 1994).

8. "Life," ix.

9. John Morgan, *Godly Learning: Puritan Attitudes towards Reason, Learning, and Education, 1560–1640* (Cambridge: Cambridge University Press, 1986), 36–106.

10. "Life," x.

11. Ibid., vi.

those within a Protestant established church."[12] Moreover, they favored a decidedly Reformed approach to theology and urged their hearers to "live according to the Reformation principles which they had already achieved legally."[13] Jonathan Moore argues that Preston's preaching was "on occasions militantly anti-Papist and anti-Arminian."[14] Not only did the content impact Preston's hearers, so too did the style. Goodwin credits Preston as the individual who transformed his own preaching style to what is known as the "plain style."[15] Goodwin's chief influences, then, were Christ-centered preachers who advocated a distinctly Reformed position on theology, the Scriptures, and the church's creeds and confessions, men who were also overtly anti-Papist and anti-Arminian.

While Goodwin was still a student at Cambridge, he prepared to receive Communion for the first time, but his hopes of participation were dashed by his only tutor at Cambridge, William Power, who refused to allow him to receive the sacrament. There is little information on Power. He did not publish any books that give clues about his theological leanings, but both extreme Puritanism and popery seem unlikely.[16] However, Power did take his duties seriously, enough so that his reason for forbidding Holy Communion to

12. Schaeffer, "The Spiritual Brotherhood," 34.

13. Ibid. For an interesting study of Preston's view on the atonement—a position that Goodwin would not adopt—see Jonathan D. Moore, *English Hypothetical Universalism: John Preston and the Softening of Reformed Theology* (Grand Rapids: Eerdmans, 2007).

14. Moore, *English Hypothetical Universalism*, 20.

15. See "Life," xiii.

16. Lawrence, "Transmission and transformation," 70.

Goodwin was most likely Goodwin's age.[17] Discouraged by this, Goodwin "left off private Prayer...and went constantly to St. Maries" to hear the "flaunting Sermons" of Richard Senhouse (*d.* 1626), whose "eloquent tongue and honest heart were capable to *over-awe a Court.*"[18] Goodwin, under the influence of Senhouse, began to lean toward Arminianism and resolved to preach against the nonconformists.

In 1617, Goodwin graduated BA, and on March 21, 1620, having received his MA from St. Catharine's College, he was elected fellow and college lecturer. Other fellows who served at St. Catharine's were John Arrowsmith, William Spurstowe, and William Strong. All would serve one day with Goodwin at the Westminster Assembly. Several of these Puritans tried to persuade Goodwin that rhetoric and Arminianism were not edifying and did not serve the truth. In addition, Goodwin could not shake the influence of Sibbes's preaching and the sermons of Preston in the college chapel.

On October 2, 1620, while listening to a funeral sermon by Thomas Bainbridge (*bap.* 1574, *d.* 1646), Goodwin underwent a conversion experience that he described as "a true work of Grace."[19] On that afternoon, he had met with some friends to have a good time. One of the friends convinced the group to attend a funeral. Bainbridge preached at that service

17. Ibid., 68.

18. J. Gauden, *Ecclesia Anglicana suspiria* (London, 1659), 614. Goodwin, speaking after his conversion, provides a fascinating comparison between the preaching of Senhouse and John Preston. See "Life," xiii.

19. Ibid., xi.

on Luke 19:41–42, focusing on the need for personal repentance. God used the message to show Goodwin his dreadful sins, the essential depravity of his heart, his averseness to all spiritual good, and his desperate condition, which left him exposed to the wrath of God. A few hours later, "before God, who after we are regenerate is so faithful and mindful of his word," Goodwin received a "speedy word" of deliverance from Ezekiel 16. He writes:

> And no Eye pitied me or could help me, but as God there (in Ezek. 16) on the sudden (for 'tis spoken as a speedy Word, as well as a vehement earnest Word, for 'tis doubled twice) yea I said unto you Live: So God was pleased on the sudden, and as it were in an instant, to alter the whole Course of his former Dispensation towards me, and so of and to my Soul, Yea live, yea live I say, said God: and as he created the World and the Matter of all things by a Word, so he created and put a new Life and Spirit into my Soul, and so great an Alteration was strange to me.
>
> God took me aside, and...privately said unto me, do you now turn to me, and I will pardon all your Sins tho never so many.... I about a Year after did expressly tell Mr Price, in declaring to him my Conversion...and I have since repeated them to others I know not how often, for they have ever stuck in my Mind.[20]

---

20. Ibid., xi. Goodwin refers to Mr. Nicholas Price as "the greatest and most famous Convert...and who was the holiest Man that ever I knew" (ibid., xii). Referring to Goodwin's conversion, William Haller described it as one of "the most notable revelations of the

Goodwin gives four reasons why he believed that "these instructions and suggestions [of deliverance and pardon] were immediately from God": (1) the condition of his heart prior to receiving the word of God's willingness to pardon—"the posture and condition of my spirit, and that this suggestion took me when my heart was fixed, and that unmoveably, in the contrary persuasions"; (2) the appropriateness of this divine word when it came—"it was a word in its proper season"; (3) that this word was "not an ungrounded fancy, but the pure word of God, which is the ground of faith and hope"; and (4) that this divine intimation had "consequents and effects after God's speaking to me," including an altered disposition of soul; a dissolution of the works of Satan; an enlightened understanding; a melted will disposed to turn to God; a new nature "inclining me to good"; the Spirit of God as "a new indweller"; and "an actual turning from all known sins, and my entertaining the truth of all godliness."[21]

Upon conversion, Goodwin aligned himself unequivocally for the remainder of his life with the theological tradition of Perkins, Sibbes, and Preston. He resolved never to seek personal fame, but "to part with all for Christ and make the glory of God the measure of all time to come."[22] Consequently, he abandoned the polished style of preaching then common among Anglican divines, since it promoted

Puritan soul" (*The Rise of Puritanism* [New York: Columbia University Press, 1957], 75).

21. "Life," xi–xiii.

22. Ibid., xii.

the preacher, and adopted the Puritan plain style of preaching, which, in its self-conscious disuse of human embellishment, sought to give all glory to God. His preaching became earnest, didactic, experimental, and pastoral.

From 1620 to 1627, Goodwin sought personal assurance of faith. Through letters and conversations with a godly minister, Rev. Nicholas Price of King's Lynn (who Goodwin said was "the greatest man for experimental acquaintance with Christ that ever he met"), he was led to see his need to "live by faith in Christ, and to derive from him life and strength for sanctification, and all comfort and joy through believing."[23] Later, he said about this time of spiritual struggle: "I was diverted from Christ for several years, to search only into the signs of grace in me. It was almost seven years ere I was taken off to live by faith on Christ, and God's free love, which are alike the object of faith."[24]

Goodwin's soul finally found rest in Christ alone. His preaching became more Christ-centered. He could agree with Sibbes's advice: "Young man, if you ever would do good, you must preach the gospel and the free grace of God in Christ Jesus."[25]

Goodwin's conversion at Cambridge marked the beginning of what is surely one of the most interesting—and longest—ecclesiastical careers in the history of English Puritanism, rivalled only by that of his fellow Independent and friend, Owen.

---

23. Ibid., xiii.

24. Ibid.

25. Ibid.

St. Andrew's the Great

(*Picture: courtesy of Cambridgeshire County Council*)

Early Career

On March 2, 1622, Goodwin was ordained a deacon at Peterborough. Three years later, having been licensed as a university preacher, he began preaching at St. Andrew's the Great. A year later, in 1626, Goodwin was influential in bringing Sibbes, "that holy and reverend Man," to be master of St Catharine's Hall.[26] Goodwin eventually became curate at St. Andrew's and in 1628 was elected to succeed Preston, who had died that year, as lecturer at Trinity Church. Preston chose Goodwin, along with Sibbes, John Davenport (*bap.* 1597, *d.* 1670), and John Ball

26. Ibid., xiv. For a good modern treatment of Sibbes's theology in the seventeenth-century context, see Mark E. Dever, *Richard Sibbes: Puritanism and Calvinism in Late Elizabethan and Early Stuart England* (Macon, Ga.: Mercer University Press, 2000).

(1585–1640), to edit his sermons.[27] While Goodwin was at Trinity, John Buckeridge (*d.* 1631), bishop of Ely, "in pursuance of the King's Proclamation," attempted to impose an oath on Goodwin "not to preach about any controverted Points in Divinity."[28] Goodwin responded, arguing that he would be left with little to preach on given that almost all points of divinity are disputed. Specifically, he made no mention of refuting Arminianism to Buckeridge, but only the "gross errors of popery." Because Goodwin subscribed to the Three Articles of Canon 36, he was admitted as lecturer and continued at Trinity Church until 1634, also serving as vicar from 1632–1634.[29]

Goodwin's resignation from Trinity Church is explained by Tom Webster in terms of Goodwin's scruples over popish ceremonies. "Samuel Hartlib," writes Webster, "reported only that Goodwin had resigned his place at Cambridge because of his changed views on ceremonies."[30] In connection with this, and based on his exegesis of Revelation 11, Goodwin's vision for the church was to purify it in

27. Besides editing Preston's sermons, Goodwin was an editor or publisher of the works of Sibbes, Jeremiah Burroughs (*bap.* 1601?, *d.* 1646), John Cotton (1585–1652), and Thomas Hooker (1586–1647).

28. "Life," xvii. Lawrence notes that it "is not clear to what Buckeridge was referring as 'the King's Proclamation'" ("Transmission and transformation," 88–94). If the proclamation spoken of is the royal Declaration, issued by Charles I, prefaced to the Thirty-Nine Articles, it would have had particular negative implications for Goodwin's Calvinistic doctrines.

29. Lawrence, "Transmission and transformation," 95; see also Halley, "Memoir," xxiv.

30. Webster, *Godly clergy in early Stuart England,* 306.

light of the eschatological age in which he lived.[31] In his opposition to Rome, Goodwin, the Puritan, saw himself as a reformer of what he hoped would become a pure Church of England.

Goodwin, convinced from his exegesis of Revelation 11 of the necessity of a second reformation, hoped to organize the Church of England "around particular congregations composed of true, or visible, saints."[32] His ecclesiology had also been re-thought in light of the influence of Cotton (1585–1652), a noted Congregationalist.[33] In 1644, Cotton entrusted Goodwin and Philip Nye (*bap.*, 1595, *d.* 1672) with the printing of his work, *The Keys of the Kingdom of Heaven* (1644). In the preface, Goodwin and Nye describe Independency as the "middle-way" between Brownism and Presbyterianism. Goodwin, then, became an Independent in England, not in Holland. However, Holland, specifically Arnhem, allowed Goodwin to put into practice what he had come to believe while in England. These facts have caused historians to view Goodwin as the founder of Congregationalism.[34] However, his views on church government must be

31. See "Revelation," in *Works*, vol. 3.

32. Lawrence, "Transmission and transformation," 113.

33. Cotton Mather records that prior to his departure for New England in 1633, John Cotton convinced Goodwin and others of Congregationalism (Cotton Mather, *Magnalia Christi Americana* [New York: Russell & Russell, 1967], 1:264–65).

34. It is important to note that terms such as "Congregationalism" and "Presbyterianism" are somewhat anachronistic prior to 1640 (see Webster, *Godly clergy*, 310–32). "Congregationalism," however, as a theological term, is useful in terms of understanding the trajectory of Goodwin's ecclesiological convictions.

understood in the context of his eschatology. The evidence from Goodwin's exegetical work on Revelation suggests that he viewed himself as a reformer of the Church of England, not a rigid separatist.[35] However, if the Church of England was going to undergo a thorough reformation, the type prophesied in Revelation 11, it would need to be done around particular, godly congregations.

Robert Halley remarks that after Goodwin left Cambridge in 1634, due to his refusal to submit to Archbishop William Laud's articles of conformity, "little more is known of him for the next five years than his marriage in 1638 to Elizabeth [Prescott]" (*d.* 1648?), a marriage that would bring him significant financial benefits and social connections.[36] Sometime in November 1638, Goodwin fled to the Netherlands and settled in Arnhem, "where he might exercise his Ministry in the Gospel, and enjoy the ordinances of Christ, according to his Conscience," which he was unable to do in England.[37] While there may be some truth that Goodwin was unwilling "to live wholly upon his wife's means, and so needed a Church to allow him maintenance,"[38] there were

35. For a discussion of the relationship between Goodwin's ecclesiology and eschatology, see Lawrence, "Transmission and transformation," 95–141.

36. Halley, "Memoir," xxiv.

37. "Life," xviii.

38. Thomas Edwards, *Antapologia* (London, 1644), 25. Edwards's *Antapologia* was the most controversial reply to the Dissenting Brethren's *An Apologetical Narration* (1644). Goodwin, Philip Nye (*bap.* 1595, *d.* 1672), Sydrach Simpson (1600–1655), William Bridge (1600/01–1671), and Burroughs were the five Independent ministers

other forces at play. Matthew Wren's (1585–1667) determined opposition to Puritanism, as the bishop of Ely (appointed March 20, 1638), and desire to ensure conformity, thus aligning himself with Charles I and William Laud, meant that Goodwin had little choice but to flee potential pursuivants. At this time, debate over the practices in worship in the Church of England intensified, leading ultimately to the Civil War in 1642.[39] Not only did the anti-Calvinists attack the Reformed doctrine of predestination, they replaced "the Calvinist emphasis on internal piety with an elaborate public worship service based on the prayer book and canons."[40] Goodwin's departure to Holland, then, not only kept him safe but allowed him to worship according to his conscience.

In Arnhem, along with Nye, Goodwin served in his first Congregational church from 1639–1641, a congregation described by Keith Sprunger as "small but vigorous."[41] Sprunger adds that the church was

---

who presented *An Apologetical Narration*, concerning matters of church government, to the Westminster Assembly.

39. As Peter Lake, Anthony Milton, and Kenneth Fincham have demonstrated, besides predestination, there were other religio-political causes that led to the Civil War in England during the seventeenth century. Their goal has been to "nudge the current historigraphical debate away from an obsessive preoccupation with one doctrine—predestination—and towards an appreciation of a range of contentious issues: conformity, order, worship, clerical authority and wealth" (Kenneth Fincham, ed., *The Early Stuart Church: 1603–1642* [Stanford: Stanford University Press, 1993], 1–2).

40. Esther Gilman Richey, *The Politics of Revelation in the English Renaissance* (Columbia: University of Missouri Press, 1998), 9.

41. Keith L. Sprunger, *Dutch Puritanism: A History of English and Scottish Churches of the Netherlands in the Sixteenth and Seventeenth Centu-*

"organized on the basis of a church covenant."[42] That is, only the "truly godly" were admitted, and only after being thoroughly examined by the whole congregation.[43] The Scottish Presbyterian Robert Baillie (1602–1662), noted for his opposition to Independency, refers to the discipline carried "in the best ruled Congregations that ever they had; that of Arnhem," as overly excessive.[44] He argues that church discipline was unnecessarily tedious: "The whole Congregation...have been forced to lay aside the works of their ordinary calling for many days of the week, to attend the judging of these causes which on the Sabbath days could not be ended."[45]

---

ries. Studies in the history of Christian thought, vol. 31 (Leiden: Brill, 1982), 226. Goodwin's ecclesiology has been the subject of a good deal of enquiry. Besides Sprunger, see Carter, "The Presbyterian-Independent controversy"; Lawrence, "Transmission and transformation"; David R. Ehalt, "The development of early congregational theory of the church with special reference to the five 'Dissenting Brethren' at the Westminster Assembly" (Ph.D. dissertation, Claremont University, 1969); J. P. Burgess, "The problem of Scripture and political affairs as reflected in the puritan revolution: Samuel Rutherford, Thomas Goodwin, John Goodwin and Gerrard Winstanley" (Ph.D. dissertation, University of Chicago, 1986); Geoffrey F. Nuttall, *Visible Saints: The Congregational Way, 1640–1660,* 2nd ed. (Weston Rhyn: Qinta Press, 2001); Murray Tolmie, *The Triumph of the Saints: The Separate Churches of London, 1616–1649* (Cambridge: Cambridge University Press, 1977), 85–106; Webster, *Godly clergy,* 305–309.

42. Sprunger, *Dutch Puritanism*, 228–29.

43. Ibid., 229. Similarly, Nuttall describes the concern for godliness as the "first principle underlying what was distinctive in Congregational thought and practise" (*Visible Saints*, 131).

44. Robert Baillie, *A Dissuasive from the Errors of the Time* (London, 1645), 122.

45. Ibid., 122–23. See also Sprunger, *Dutch Puritanism*, 229.

Halley is surely correct in arguing that during this time Goodwin and Nye appear to have arrived at their definitive convictions about church order and discipline, convictions "which they afterwards clearly stated, and ably defended, in the *Apologetical Narration.*"[46] Goodwin's plan for reformation was not yet realized, but the next two decades would see him involved in ongoing attempts to reform the Church of England along more thoroughly biblical lines in terms of ecclesiology (i.e., Independency) and soteriology (i.e., Calvinism) in fulfillment of the eschatological promises of Revelation 11, leading to a church where the Scriptures would be "alone a sufficient Rule to square Churches (both Worshippers and Worship)."[47]

The Westminster Assembly

Sometime in 1641, Goodwin returned to England to be a pastor of a church in London. In 1643, "by an ordinance of Parliament," he was "appointed to be a Member of the venerable Assembly of Divines at Westminster."[48] His son Thomas evidently did not feel that Goodwin's role at the Westminster Assembly was particularly noteworthy to readers of the "Life" and so proceeds to speak about Cotton's invitation to Goodwin, in 1647, to come to New England.[49] However, Goodwin's involvement at the Westminster

46. Halley, "Memoir," xxvi.

47. Goodwin, "Revelation," *Works*, 3:118.

48. "Life," xviii.

49. Lawrence provides a fascinating analysis of the "editorial sins of omission" by Goodwin's son in the "Life" ("Transmission and transformation," 215–17).

Assembly is particularly important in terms of understanding him in his seventeenth-century context. The context of the Civil War saw Goodwin engaged at the Westminster Assembly in what proved to be a failed attempt to reform the Church of England.[50]

What little is known from Thomas Goodwin Jr. about his father's time at the Assembly is that Goodwin, in the debates on church government, argued "with such Modesty and Christian Meekness, that it procured the Esteem of those who differed from him, and the other dissenting Brethren in their Judgment."[51] However, the recent work of Chad Van Dixhoorn, which includes the *Minutes* of the Westminster Assembly, sheds important light on Goodwin's activities during the 1640s.[52] Goodwin played a major role at the Assembly, not only in ecclesiological debates but in theological ones, especially those focusing on the doctrine of justification.[53] Historiography on the Assembly, up until Van Dixhoorn's thesis, focused almost exclusively on ecclesiological debates without

---

50. Among the best treatments of the English Civil War and the events leading up to it are Peter Gaunt, *The English Civil War: The Essential Readings* (Oxford: Blackwell Publishers, 2000); John S. Morrill, *The Impact of the English Civil War* (London: Collins & Brown, 1991); Nicholas Tyacke, *Anti-Calvinists: The Rise of English Arminianism, c. 1590–1640* (Oxford: Oxford University Press, 1987); Anthony Milton, *Catholic and Reformed: The Roman and Protestant Churches in English Protestant Thought, 1600–1640* (Cambridge: Cambridge University Press, 1995).

51. "Life," xviii.

52. See Chad Van Dixhoorn, "Reforming the Reformation: Theological Debate at the Westminster Assembly 1643–1652, Volumes 1–7" (Ph.D. dissertation, Cambridge University, 2004).

53. For example, see ibid., 1:270–344.

giving due attention to other important theological disputes. Van Dixhoorn has argued persuasively that theology "is the most neglected area in Assembly historiography."[54] In fact, the assumption has often been that debates over church government slowed the Assembly down, while debates over other doctrinal matters provided smooth sailing. But smooth sailing it was not. It is a striking fact that some divines were concerned about the ecclesiology of the Independents and their proximity to schismatics, but only when debating Christology did the divines call each other heretics. In a similar vein, while some divines thought that Presbyterianism was only a small step away from prelacy and Romanism, only when debating justification did they accuse one another of popery.[55]

Records of the Assembly covering 243 sessions held from August 1643 to December 1644 indicate that Goodwin gave more addresses than any other divine—357 in all![56] In line with the goals of the Assembly, Goodwin saw himself carrying on his life project, the reformation of the Church of England along godly lines with respect to both ecclesiology and Reformed orthodoxy. However, the *Minutes* of the Westminster Assembly indicate that despite Goodwin's best efforts, along with fellow Indepen-

54. Ibid., 1:8. Subsequent chapters will show how Goodwin's prominence in theological debates at the Westminster Assembly shed further light on his Christology.

55. Ibid., 1:348.

56. Wayne R. Spear, "Covenanted Uniformity in Religion: The Influence of the Scottish Commissioners Upon the Ecclesiology of the Westminster Assembly" (Ph.D. dissertation, University of Pittsburgh, 1976), 362.

dents, to compose an *Apollogeticall Narration* (1644) and *A Copy of a Remonstrance Lately Delivered in the Assembly* (1645), Presbyterianism triumphed.[57] Consequently, Goodwin's role at the Assembly decreased markedly thereafter, though in 1647, along with Jeremiah Walker, he oversaw the printing of the Assembly's papers.

The Interregnum

With the regicide of Charles I in 1649, Goodwin, along with Owen and Nye, became a principal architect of the Cromwellian church. Goodwin preached before the House of Commons on June 7 of that year. On January 8, 1650, Parliament appointed Goodwin to the presidency of Magdalen College, Oxford, where he preached every second week, alternating with Owen, at St. Mary's.[58] Toward the end of the year, he was made D.D. of Oxford. Goodwin also pastored a church at this time that included "good Men though of different Persuasions," such as Independents Thankful Owen (1620–1681), Theophilus

57. For Goodwin's role in the Presbyterian-Independent controversy, see Fienberg, "Thomas Goodwin: Puritan Pastor and Independent Divine," 80–265; Brent Gustafsson, *The Five Dissenting Brethren: A Study of the Dutch Background of Their Independentism* (London: C. W. K. Gloerup, 1955); R. B. Carter, "The Presbyterian-Independent Controversy with Special Reference to Dr. Thomas Goodwin and the Years 1640 to 1660" (Ph.D. dissertation, University of Edinburgh, 1961); Ehalt, "The Development of Early Congregational Theory of the Church with Special Reference to the Five 'Dissenting Brethren' at the Westminster Assembly"; John R. DeWitt, *Jus Divinum: The Westminster Assembly and the Divine Right of Church Government* (Kampen: Kok, 1962).

58. Halley, "Memoir," xxvii–xxxiv.

Magdalen College, of which Goodwin was appointed president in 1650

Gale (1628–1679), and Stephen Charnock (1628–1680), the Presbyterian John Howe (1630–1705),[59] and Zachary Mayne (1631–1694), who struggled with Arian and Socinian views, though he later gave evidence that he renounced these heretical positions in *The Snare Broken* (1692) and *Sanctification by Faith Vindicated* (1693).

Goodwin's influence shaped Magdalen College into an institution known for adherence to scriptural truth and Calvinistic, experimental doctrine. Demanding academic excellence and dealing plainly with the spiritual lives of the students, Goodwin was soon accused of operating a "scruple shop" by those

59. Halley records that Howe had initially prevented himself from uniting to the church where Goodwin pastored. However, "Goodwin…readily agreed to admit him upon liberal and catholic grounds to the privileges of their society. This is one of many proofs that Goodwin was not that narrow and bigoted sectary which he has been often represented" (ibid., xxxv).

who did not appreciate his Puritan emphasis on intelligent piety. In those years, however, as even Lord Clarendon later admitted, "the University of Oxford yielded a harvest of extraordinary good and sound knowledge in all parts of learning."[60]

Goodwin's labors at Oxford during the 1650s marked a time of blessing for students who would later become Protestant nonconformists. Philip Henry (1631–1696), according to his son, Matthew Henry (1662–1714), often spoke of the "great helps and advantages he had then in the University, not only for learning, but for religion and piety. Serious godliness was in reputation, and besides the public opportunities they had, there were many of the scholars that used to meet together for prayer, and Christian conference to the great confirmation of one another's hearts in the fear and love of God and the preparing of them for the service of the Church in their generation."[61]

The 1650s, then, was a unique time in Oxford's history. It was noted as a center of Anglicanism from the days of Henry VIII, and, after the brief rule of the Cromwells, has been Anglican since the Restoration. However, at the time, Goodwin surely hoped that his vision for true reformation in the English church was taking place. That context explains Goodwin's actions during the Interregnum, a period that saw Goodwin at the height of his ecclesiastical and political activity.

---

60. Cited in Peter Toon, *Puritans and Calvinism* (Swengel, Pa.: Reiner, 1973), 47.

61. Matthew Henry, *An Account of the Life and Death of Mr. Philip Henry* (London, 1699), 19.

With the passing of the Act of Oblivion—an act that granted pardon for acts of treason against the Commonwealth committed before September 3, 1651—the Socinian John Biddle (1616–1662) was released from prison on February 10, 1652. Goodwin was among fifteen Independent ministers who appeared before the House of Commons with a petition in an attempt to thwart the threat posed by Biddle's doctrines, which included a denial of "the Trinity, the divinity of Christ, [and] the divinity of the Holy Spirit."[62] Biddle, according to Lawrence, "was the motivation for the first of three confessions of faith which Goodwin helped draft in the 1650s."[63] Biddle's *Socinian Catechesis ecclesiarum*, known as the Racovian Catechism, was countered by *The Humble Proposals of Mr. Owen, Mr. Tho. Goodwin, Mr. Nye, Mr. Sympson, and other Ministers* (March 31, 1652). The *Proposals* was followed by the *Principles of Christian Religion*, published later that year. Richard Baxter (1615–1691) charged the Independents with extreme factionalism given the content of the *Proposals* and *Principles*. However, Lawrence has argued that the *Proposals*, for example, "gives every indication of being a compromise document."[64] For example, it granted far more authority to extra-congregational authorities than previous Independent statements on church government had allowed. At the same time, the commissions created were but a shadow of

62. John H. McLachlan, *Socinianism in Seventeenth-Century England* (Oxford: Oxford University Press, 1951), 188.

63. Lawrence, "Transmission and transformation," 144.

64. Ibid., 150.

what the Assembly of Divines at Westminster had intended. Nevertheless, there was something in the *Proposals* for both sides to cheer, and one is left with the distinct impression that what made both Presbyterian and Independent favorably disposed towards them was their potential to bring the sects firmly to heel. Here was a common cause and a common vehicle which had the potential to reunite Puritans on both sides of the ecclesiological divide.

Notwithstanding the fact that these documents were ecumenical in terms of the Independent-Presbyterian divide, they were intended to safeguard the orthodoxy of the Christian faith. Hence, the Socinians, Quakers, pantheists, and antinomians were excluded on grounds of heresy.[65] Not surprisingly, the *Proposals* and *Principles* were met with strong opposition by those condemned, and the Rump managed to approve only three of the proposals before its dissolution.

With the establishment of the Protectorate in February 1654, Oliver Cromwell made Goodwin, along with a mixed group of Independent and Presbyterians, such as Baxter, Owen, Francis Cheynell (1608–1665), Thomas Manton (1620–1677), Nye, and Sidrach Simpson (c. 1600–1655), a participant in a parliamentary conference designed to write a confession of faith for the Cromwellian church.[66] The result was *A New Confession of Faith, or the first*

---

65. Lawrence notes that the language toward the antinomians is stronger in the *Principles* than in the *Westminster Confession of Faith* ("Transmission and transformation," 161).

66. For an excellent discussion of this conference, see ibid., 166–82.

Principles of the Christian Religion necessary to be laid as a Foundation by all such as desire to build on unto Perfection (1654).[67] *A New Confession*, like the *Principles* (1652), followed the outline of the Apostles' Creed. The content followed Nicene Trinitarianism, Chalcedonian Christology, and Calvinistic soteriology. However, while similarities between the two aforementioned confessions are obvious, there are some important differences. Subscribing to the *New Confession* was more difficult for Arminians and "those whose understanding of justification strayed from the standard laid out by the Westminster Divines," such as Baxter.[68] *A New Confession*, containing twenty articles of faith, was presented to Parliament on December 12, 1654.[69] Unfortunately for Goodwin, as in 1652, Parliament was dissolved before it could discuss the merits of *A New Confession* and its proposed consequences for heretical groups.

No doubt Goodwin was disappointed over the dissolution of Parliament, which seemed likely to frustrate further attempts to reform the church during the Interregnum. However, the era of the Protectorate represented a time of prosperity for the Independents. Having spent the preceding years perfecting some of his writings, Goodwin, along with fellow Independents, secured Oliver Cromwell's (reluctant) permission to convene a synod and draft the *Savoy*

---

67. Lawrence notes that the "sole extant copy is in the Thomason Collection.... Thomason noted that it was presented to parliament on 12 December 1654" (ibid., 170).

68. Ibid., 172.

69. Ibid., 181.

Declaration (1658). On September 29, 1658, Goodwin, along with Owen, Nye, William Bridge (1600–1671), and William Greenhill (1598–1671)—all of whom, except for Owen, had participated at the Westminster Assembly—drew up the new statement of faith. It was almost identical to the *Westminster Confession of Faith* except in the area of ecclesiology, though several seemingly minor differences are important in understanding certain nuances of Goodwin's Christology.[70] The *Savoy Declaration* was immensely influential in both British and American Congregationalism, becoming the confessional standard for Independent churches on both continents.

On September 3, 1658, the anniversary of the "eminent mercy" at Dunbar (1650) and the "crowning mercy" of Worcester (1651)—major victories for Cromwell and the Parliamentary forces—Goodwin attended Cromwell's deathbed. Cromwell had a moment of misgiving, perhaps due to his various life experiences, and asked Goodwin whether the doctrine of the saints' perseverance were true, that is, that the elect could never fall away from the faith. "Nothing could be more certain" was Goodwin's response. "Then I am safe," said Cromwell, "for I am sure that once I was in a state of grace!"[71] Cromwell knew that his hour had come to die, but Goodwin did not seem to think so.[72] Cromwell died minutes later, however,

70. There are some other, more subtle, differences that fall beyond the scope of this chapter.

71. Eliakim Littell and Robert S. Littell, *The Living Age* (New York: Living Age Co., 1845), 112.

72. Halley, "Memoir," xxxvii.

and so, too, in some respects, did Goodwin's Puritan vision for the Church of England.

Cromwell was succeeded as lord protector by his son Richard (1626–1712). Richard lacked the necessary power base in both Parliament and the army to continue as lord protector. He was forced to resign in May 1659, bringing the Protectorate to an end. This was not only the end for the Cromwellian church, but the end of both Goodwin's public career and his efforts to reform and defend the Church of England.

The Restoration

The English monarchy was restored on May 8, 1660. Parliament, both Lords and Commons, insisted that Charles II became king on January 30, 1649; "they were only now finding opportunity to proclaim that fact."[73] Religion, as in the Cromwellian church, remained very much at the forefront in the Restoration period.[74] Goodwin's public career, however, ended with his resignation from Magdalen College on May 9, 1660.[75]

Goodwin's resignation ushered in a "retired Life, spent in Prayer, Reading and Meditation."[76] Goodwin, however, hoped to secure religious toleration as he retired to London with many of his Oxford congregation. The Act of Uniformity (1662) imposed

---

73. Lawrence, "Transmission and transformation," 9.

74. Diana Newton, *Papists, Protestants, and Puritans, 1559–1714* (Cambridge: Cambridge University Press, 1998), 62.

75. See Lawrence, "Transmission and transformation," 9; W. D. Macray, *A Register of the Members of St. Mary Magdalen College, Oxford: from the foundation of the College* (Oxford, 1904), 4:7; "Life," xviii.

76. Ibid.

"unequivocal acceptance of its content" on Puritans like Goodwin.[77] Moreover, public pulpits and both universities were no longer open to them.[78] Lawrence rightly notes the psychological impact of the Act of Uniformity on nonconformists such as Goodwin:

> Men who had been trained to preach and teach, men who had spent a lifetime developing the rhetorical tools necessary to persuade a nation to godliness, were by this act forbidden to do the very thing for which they lived. Adding injury to insult, the harsh sanctions of the Clarendon Code were soon enacted to enforce their silence. Cut off from both public life and public worship, Goodwin did not simply withdraw to the tranquil world of the pastor's study. Rather, he was forced into the quietly furtive life of the nonconformist minister, managing his affairs in order to avoid confrontation with the authorities.[79]

The Restoration settlement of the church, begun in 1660, was followed by almost thirty years of persecution. For the remainder of his life, Goodwin would never enjoy the religious liberty he did during the Interregnum.

In light of the changing circumstances in Goodwin's life, historians have argued that most of Goodwin's collected *Works* were written within the context of the Restoration.[80] Among such historians

---

77. Newton, *Papists, Protestants, and Puritans*, 63.

78. Lawrence, "Transmission and transformation," 11.

79. Ibid.

80. For example, see Christopher Hill, *The Experience of Defeat: Milton and Some Contemporaries* (London: Faber, 1984), 65.

is Christopher Hill, who has argued that Goodwin's writings were his response to the bitter experience of defeat. Lawrence's work, on the other hand, clearly demonstrates that the *Works* are representative of "the thought of a puritan divine across the span of his career, and not simply at the end of it."[81]

The persecution of nonconformists sparked an exodus to New England. As noted previously, Goodwin was reported to have been invited by Cotton to immigrate to New England, but Goodwin's second wife, Mary (1632–1693), whom he married in 1649 shortly after the death of his first wife, Elizabeth, convinced him to stay, according to John Davenport. Goodwin, like Owen, because of his former ecclesiastical and political prominence and various social connections, does not appear to have suffered to the same degree under the Clarendon Code as many other nonconformists. Unlike Thomas Jollie (1629–1703), who was imprisoned five times, and John Bunyan (1628–1688), Goodwin did not spend time inside a jail. Nonconformists in London seem to have benefited from a general reluctance to enforce the Clarendon code.[82] Goodwin even spoke on behalf of Congregational ministers before Charles II on February 27, 1663. Goodwin appears to have taken the king's advice to meet inconspicuously in order to avoid the various penalties enforced on nonconformists at the time.

---

81. Lawrence, "Transmission and transformation," 51. See the foregoing discussion in the "Status Quaestionis" regarding Lawrence's findings on the dating of Goodwin's *Works*.

82. Fienberg, "Puritan Pastor and Independent Divine," 343.

The Great Fire (1666), which destroyed part of Goodwin's library

Goodwin, then, continued to minister to his congregation in London, even through the Great Plague (1665–1666). Nearly seventy thousand deaths resulted from the plague, and there would have been more if thousands had not fled London. Among those who fled was Owen, who left London for Stoke Newington. Baxter surmises that Owen deliberately left London, and his gathered church, during the plague. Baxter's implication seems to be that Owen should have stayed and cared for his people during this time, like many other heroic nonconformist ministers.[83] Regardless of the propriety or lack thereof of Owen's actions, there was a growing sentiment among nonconformists that the plague and Great Fire (1666)

83. Richard Baxter, *Reliquiæ Baxterianæ, or, Mr. Richard Baxter's Narrative of the Most Memorable Passages of His Life and Times* (London, 1696), Pt. III, 19. Baxter confirms that Goodwin and Nye were the nonconformist leaders in London at this time.

were signs of God's judgment on England for the oppressive attitude toward nonconformity.

Thomas Goodwin Jr., the inheritor of his father's great library, laments the consequences of the second disaster in London that year:

> In that deplorable Calamity of the dreadful Fire at London, 1666, which laid in Ashes a considerable part of that City, he [Thomas Goodwin, Sr.] lost above half his Library, to the value of five hundred Pounds. There was this remarkable [thing], that part of it, which was lodged very near the Place where the Fire began, and which he accounted irrecoverably lost, were by the good Providence of God, and the Care and Diligence of his very good and faithful Friend Mr. Moses Lowman, though with extreme hazard, preserved from the Flames.[84]

Goodwin, according to his son Thomas, admitted that God had "struck him in a very sensible Place" because he loved his library so much. Fortunately for Goodwin, his divinity books, "which were chiefly of use to him," were preserved.[85]

In the years between 1662 and 1672, Goodwin appears to have lived quietly. He published only *Patience and its Perfect Work* (1666), and that anonymously. From about 1672 to the end of his life, Goodwin, licensed as a Congregational minister, was in poor health. In a letter to Robert Asty sometime around May 1675, Goodwin excuses himself for not

84. "Life," xix.

85. Ibid., xix. See also Halley, "Memoir," xxxix.

responding sooner due to being "weak and sickish."[86] Finally, in February 1680, "a Fever seized him, which in a few Days put an end to his Life."[87] Goodwin died on the eighteenth day of that month, having lived almost eighty years amid some of the most remarkable events in England's ecclesiastical and political history. His closing exhortation to his two sons was to "value the Privilege of the Covenant."[88] Thomas Goodwin Jr. wrote of his godly father:

> In all the violence of [his fever], he discoursed with that strength of faith and assurance of Christ's love, with that holy admiration of free grace, with that joy in believing, and such thanksgivings and praises, as he extremely moved and affected all that heard him.... He rejoiced in the thoughts that he was dying, and going to have a full and uninterrupted communion with God. 'I am going,' said he, 'to the three Persons, with whom I have had communion: they have taken me; I did not take them.... I could not have imagined I should ever have had such a measure of faith in this hour.... Christ cannot love me better than he doth; I think I cannot love Christ better than I do; I am swallowed up in God....' With this assurance of faith, and fullness of joy, his soul left this world.[89]

Goodwin attained recognition as a leader of Independency during the Civil War and the Interreg-

86. *Works*, 4:51.

87. "Life," xix.

88. Ibid., xix.

89. Goodwin Jr., "Memoir," 2:lxxiv–lxxxv.

Thomas Goodwin's grave
(*Photograph: Marty Foord*)

num period, and was also known among the Puritan divines of the seventeenth century as an eminent believer, an able preacher, a caring pastor, and a profoundly spiritual writer. Buried in Bunhill Fields, his epitaph, written in Latin, is most moving when read in full. It summarizes well his most important gifts, stating that he was knowledgeable in the Scriptures, sound in judgment, and enlightened by the Spirit to penetrate the mysteries of the gospel; he was a pacifier of troubled consciences, a dispeller of error, and a truly Christian pastor; he edified many souls whom he had first won to Christ. The closing section of his epitaph has been repeatedly fulfilled through the centuries by the reprinting of his works:

> His writings…, the noblest monument of this great man's praise, will diffuse his name in a more

> fragrant odour than that of the richest perfume, to flourish in those distant ages, when this marble, inscribed with his just honour, shall have dropt into dust.[90]

Christological Piety

More than anything else, Goodwin excelled in promoting Christological piety, as the excerpts from his writings in this book show. Halley sums it up best:

> Of his fervent piety I need say nothing. His life is his "epistle of commendation." And if that be not sufficient, "he being dead, yet speaketh" by his numerous practical and experimental writings, in which the sanctified thoughts and emotions of a renewed heart are expressed in appropriate words of truth and soberness.[91]

As you read this book, we pray that Goodwin's Christ-centered piety may penetrate you and spur you on to read more of his writings, so that you might "grow in grace, and in the knowledge of our Lord and Saviour Jesus Christ. To him be glory both now and for ever. Amen" (2 Peter 3:18).

---

90. Halley, "Memoir," xliii.

91. Halley, "Memoir," xlvi.

John Cotton (1585–1652)

Puritan, ministered in New England. Cotton convinced Goodwin of congregational polity, entrusted him with publishing one of his books, and had even encouraged him to move to New England.

1

Christ Excels Joseph[1]

Now when Christ comes first out of the other world, from the dead, clothed with that heart and body which He was to wear in heaven, what message does He send first to them? We would all think that as they would not know Him in His sufferings, so He would now be as strange to them in His glory; or at least that His first words would be to berate them for their faithlessness and falsehood. But here is no such matter, for His first word concerning them is, "Go tell my brethren..." (John 20:17). You read elsewhere how it is a great point of love and condescension in Christ so to entitle them. Hebrews 2:11 says, "He is not ashamed to call them brethren," though surely His brethren had been ashamed of Him. For Him to call them so when He is first entering into His glory argues the more love in Him toward them. He carries it as Joseph did in the height of his advancement, when he first opened his mind to his brethren; "I am Joseph your brother," he said (Gen. 45:4). So Christ says here, "Tell them you have seen Jesus their brother; I own them as brethren still." But what is the message that He would first have delivered to them?

1. From *The Heart of Christ in Heaven Towards Sinners on Earth; Works* 4:104–105.

"That I," says He, "ascend to my Father, and *your* Father" (John 20:17).

This is a more friendly speech by far, and argues infinitely more love than that of Joseph (though his was full of compassion), for Joseph, after he had told them he was their brother, added, "whom you sold into Egypt"; he reminded them of their unkindness. Not so Christ. He says not a word of that; He reminds them not of what they had done against Him. Poor sinners, who are full of the thoughts of their own sins, know not how they shall be able at the latter day to look Christ in the face when they shall first meet with Him. But they may relieve their spirits against this care and fear by Christ's conduct toward His disciples, who had so sinned against Him. Be not afraid, your sins He will remember no more.

Yea, further, you may observe that He reminds them not so much of what He had been doing for them. He says not, "Tell them I have been dying for them" or "They little think what I have suffered for them"; not a word of that either. His heart and His care are set upon doing more: He looks not backward to what is passed, but forgets His sufferings, as a woman her travail, for joy that a man-child is born. Having now dispatched that great work on earth for them, He hastens to heaven as fast as He can to do another. And though He knows He has business yet to do upon earth that will hold Him forty days longer, yet to show that His heart is longing and eagerly desirous to be at work for them in heaven, He speaks in the present tense and tells them, "I ascend"; and He expresses His joy that, not only does He go to *His* Father, but that He goes to *their* Father, to be an advocate with Him for them, of which I spoke before. And is indeed Jesus our brother alive? And does He call us brethren? And does He talk thus lovingly of us? Whose heart would not this overcome?

William Perkins (1558–1602)

Influential Puritan, taught at Cambridge University. Goodwin wrote that when he entered Cambridge, six of his instructors who had sat under Perkins were still passing on his teaching.

2

Christ Longs for His Own Return[1]

It is the manner of bridegrooms, when they have made all ready in their fathers' houses, then to come themselves and fetch their brides, and not to send for them by others, because it is a time of love. Love descends better than it ascends, and so does the love of Christ, who indeed is love itself, and therefore comes down to us Himself. "I will come again and receive you unto myself," says Christ, "that so where I am, you may be also." That last part of His speech gives the reason of it and shows His entire affection. It is as if He had said, "The truth is, I cannot live without you and I shall never be quiet till I have you where I am, that we may never part again; that is the reason of it. Heaven shall not hold Me, nor My Father's company, if I do not have you with Me, My heart is so set upon you; and if I have any glory, you shall have part of it."

So, John 4:19 says, "Because I live, ye shall live also." It is a reason, and it is half an oath besides. *As I live* is God's oath; *because I live*, says Christ. He pawns His life upon it and desires to live upon no other terms; "He shall live to see his seed," etc. (Isa. 53).

1. From *The Heart of Christ in Heaven Towards Sinners on Earth; Works* 4:100.

And yet farther, the more to express the workings and longings of His heart after them all that while, He tells them it shall not be long before He comes again to them. So, "Again a little while and ye shall see me; a little while and ye shall not see me," says He (John 16:16). Not seeing Him refers not to that small space of absence while He was dead and in the grave, but to that after His last ascending, forty days after His resurrection, when He should go away, not to be seen on earth again until the day of judgment; and yet from that ascension, but "a little while," says He, "and you shall see me again," namely, at the day of judgment. It is said, "Yet a little while, and he that shall come will come, and will not tarry" (Heb. 10:37). The words in the Greek mean, "As little little as may be." Though the time is long in itself, yet it is as little while as may be in respect of His desire, without the least delaying to come. He will stay not a moment longer than till He has dispatched all our business there for us.

The doubling of the phrase, "coming he will come" (John 14:18), implies vehemency of desire to come, and that His mind is always upon it; He is still a-coming; He can hardly be kept away. Thus, the Hebrew phrase likewise signifies an urgency, vehemency, and intenseness of some act, as expecting I have expected, desiring I have desired, so coming He will come. And not content with these expressions of desire, He adds over and above all these, "and will not tarry"; and all to signify the infinite ardency of His mind toward His elect below, and to have all His elect in heaven about Him. He will not stay a minute longer than He must; He tarries only till He has throughout the ages by His intercession prepared every room for each saint, that He may entertain them all at once together and have them all about Him.

Zacharias Ursinus (1534–1583)

German Reformer, known as an author of the Heidelberg Catechism. Goodwin was introduced to Ursinus's work at Cambridge.

3

Sitting in Heaven[1]

Observe now, He is said to sit there (in heaven) over all things, not in His own pure personal right simply—it is His inheritance, as He is the Son of God (as Heb. 1:3, 4, 5, it is affirmed of Him)—but as a head to the church (Eph. 1:22). The phrase "over all things" comes between His being a head and "to the church" to show that He is set over all in relation to His church. So we see that our relation is involved and our right included in this exaltation of His. He sits not simply as a Son but as a head, and He sits not as a head without a body, so He therefore must have His members up to Him. For this reason, in the next verse it is added, "which is his body, yea, his fulness" (Eph. 1:23). So Christ is not complete without all His members and would leave heaven if any one were missing. It would be a lame, maimed body if it lacked but a toe. Christ is our element, and because He has ascended, we are sparks that fly upward to Him. He took our flesh and carried it into heaven, and left us His Spirit on earth, both being pawns and earnests that we should follow.

Furthermore, He is not only said to sit as our head, but we are said to "sit together with him." That is made the upshot of all in the next chapter

1. From *Christ Set Forth; Works* 4:53–54.

(Eph. 2:6). So just as we arose with Him, He being considered as a common person, and ascended with Him, as was said, so we sit together with Him in the highest heavens, that is, "in His exalted estate above the heavens." Not that Christ's being at God's right hand (if taken for that sublimity of power) is communicable to us; that is Christ's prerogative only.

So, "to which of all the angels did he ever say, Sit thou at my right hand?" (Heb. 1:5). Yet since His sitting in heaven, as it is indefinitely expressed, is understood to be in our right and stead, and as a common person, and so is to assure us of our sitting there with Him, in our proportion, so it is expressly rendered as the mind and intendment of it: "Him that overcometh, I will grant to sit with me in my throne, even as I also am set down with my Father in his throne" (Rev. 3:21). There is a proportion observed, though with an inequality; we sit on Christ's throne, but He alone on His Father's throne; that is, Christ alone sits at God's right hand, but we on Christ's right hand, and so the church is said to be at Christ's "right hand" (Ps. 45:9).

Furthermore (and it may afford a further comfort to us on this point), this shows that at the latter day we shall sit as assessors on His judgment seat, to judge the world with Him. "When the Son of man shall sit in his glory, ye shall sit upon twelve thrones, judging the tribes of Israel" (Matt. 19:28; Luke 22:30). Since our sitting with Him is spoken of in respect to judgment and to giving the sentence of it, not a sentence shall pass without your votes. So you may by faith not only look on yourselves as already in heaven, sitting with Christ as a common person in your right, you may look on yourselves as judges also; if any sin should arise to accuse or condemn, it must be with your votes. What greater security can you have than this? For you must condemn yourselves if you be condemned; you may very well say, "Who shall accuse? Who shall condemn?" for you will never pronounce a fatal sentence upon yourselves.

Just as Paul triumphed here, so may we, for at the present we sit in heaven with Christ and have all our enemies under our feet. As Joshua made his servants set their feet on the necks of those five kings, so God would have us by faith to do the same to all of ours, for one day we shall do it. And if you say, We see it not, I answer that the apostle says of Christ Himself, "Now we see not yet all things put under him" (Heb. 2:8). All things are not yet under Him, for He now sits in heaven and *expects* by faith that the day will come when His enemies shall be made His footstool (Heb. 10:12–13). "But we see" for the present "Jesus crowned with glory and honour" (v. 9), and so may be sure that the thing is as good as done. And in seeing Him thus crowned, we may see ourselves sitting with Him, and quietly wait and expect, as Christ Himself does, for all things to be accomplished, when our salvation will be finished and fully perfected.

Richard Sibbes (1577–1635)

Puritan at Cambridge, known as "the heavenly doctor," due to his godly preaching and manner of life. Sibbes's preaching and teaching were formative in Goodwin's life.

4

Crying Us into Heaven[1]

> "And to Jesus the mediator of the new covenant, and to the blood of sprinkling, that speaketh better things than that of Abel."
>
> —Hebrews 12:24

Christ's blood in its cry has attributed to it here a further advantage over Abel's blood. For Abel's cried only from earth, from the ground, where it lay shed, and it cried only for an answerable earthly punishment on Cain, as he was a man on the earth. But Christ's blood is carried up to heaven, for as the high priest carried the blood of the sacrifices into the Holy of Holies, so Christ has virtually carried His blood into heaven (Heb. 9:12). This is intimated here in Hebrews 12 also, as the coherence shows. For all the other particulars (of which this is one) to which he says the saints are come are in heaven. "You are come," says he, "to the city of the living God, the heavenly Jerusalem, and to an innumerable company of angels, to the church of the first-born who are written in heaven, and to God the judge of all, and to the spirits of just men made perfect" (Heb. 12:22–23). All these things are in heaven; He names nothing that is not there. He then adds, "and to the blood of sprinkling, which speaks...," as a thing that speaks in heaven and is

1. From *Christ Set Forth; Works* 4:77–78.

sprinkled from heaven, yea, a thing with which all heaven is sprinkled, as the mercy seat in the Holy of Holies was, because sinners are to come there. This blood therefore cries from heaven; it is next to God, who sits as Judge there, and it cries in His very ears, whereas the cry of blood from the ground is further off. So though the cry of blood from the ground may come up to heaven, yet the blood itself does not come there, as Christ already is there. Abel's blood cried for vengeance to come down from heaven, but Christ's blood cries us up into heaven. . . .

In the second place, add to this Christ's intercession, which was the second thing propounded—that Christ by His prayers seconds this cry of His blood. So not only does the blood of Christ cry, but Christ Himself, being alive, joins with it. How forcible and prevalent must all this be! The blood of a slain man cries, though the man remains dead, even as it is said of Abel (though to another purpose) that "being dead he yet speaketh" (Heb. 11:4). But Christ lives and appears. He follows the suit and pursues the hue and cry of His blood Himself. His being alive puts a life into His death. It is not in this case as it was in the first Adam's sin and disobedience. Adam, although he himself had been annihilated when he died, set the stock of human nature to the propagation of children. But his sin would have defiled and condemned them to the end of the world, and the force of it to condemn was neither furthered nor lessened by his subsisting and being, or by his not being; it received no assistance from his personal life one way or other. The reason is that his sin condemns us in a natural and necessary way. But the death of Christ and His shed blood save us in a way of grace and favor unto Christ Himself and for His sake. Thus, Christ, who shed this blood, being alive, adds an infinite acceptation to it with God, and moves Him the more to hear the cry of it and to regard it.

John Preston (1587–1628)

Puritan at Cambridge, whose preaching style greatly influenced Goodwin's. On his death bed, Preston chose Goodwin as one of four editors to publish his writings.

5

Christ's Gift[1]

Let us consider what Christ did when He came to heaven and was exalted there. He abundantly made good all that He had promised in His last sermon! He instantly poured out His Spirit, and that "richly" (as the apostle speaks to Titus). "Being by the right hand of God exalted, and having received of the Father the promise of the Holy Ghost, he hath shed forth this which you now see and hear," says the apostle in his first sermon after (Acts 2:33). He received the Spirit and visibly poured Him out. So Paul tells us that Christ ascended up on high, giving gifts unto men for the work of the ministry and for the jointing in of the saints to the increase of the body of Christ (Eph. 4:8, 12, 16). That is, He gave gifts for converting elect sinners and making them saints. Some of the gifts there mentioned remain to this day, including "pastors and teachers," etc. And this Spirit is still in our preaching and in your hearts, in hearing, in praying, etc., and persuades you of Christ's love to this very day. In all these things He is the pledge of the continuance of Christ's love to sinners.

All our sermons and your prayers are evidences to you that Christ's heart is still the same toward sinners

---

1. From *The Heart of Christ in Heaven Towards Sinners on Earth; Works* 4:107.

as ever, for the Spirit that assists in all these works comes in His name and in His stead, and works all by commission from Him. Do none of you feel your hearts moved in the preaching of these things, at this and other times? Who is it that moves you? It is the Spirit, who speaks in Christ's name from heaven, even as He Himself is said to "speak from heaven" (Heb. 12:25). When you pray, it is the Spirit who incites your prayers and makes intercession for you in your own hearts (Rom. 8:26)—intercession that is the evidence and echo of Christ's intercession in heaven. *The Spirit prays in you because Christ prays for you.* He is an intercessor on earth because Christ is an intercessor in heaven. Just as the Spirit took and used Christ's words that He had uttered before when He spoke in and to the disciples the words of life, so He takes Christ's prayers also when He prays in us; He takes the words, as it were, out of Christ's mouth, or rather His heart, and directs our hearts to offer them up to God. He also follows us to the sacrament, and in that mirror shows us Christ's face smiling on us, and through His face, His heart. Having thus received a sight of Him, we go away rejoicing that we saw our Savior that day.

6

Christ Dwelling in Our Hearts by Faith[1]

What is it to have Christ dwell in the heart by faith?...

First, it is to have Jesus Christ continually in one's eye, a habitual sight of Him. I call it so because a man actually does not always think of Christ; but as a man does not look up to the sun continually, yet he sees the light of it, so here faith is called the seeing of Christ: "Every one that seeth the Son, and believeth on him" (John 6:40). And our Lord and Savior Jesus Christ, speaking of Himself, says, "I have set the LORD always before me" (Ps. 16:8a). So you should carry along and bear along in your eye the sight and knowledge of Christ, so that at least a presence of Him accompanies you, which faith makes.

Second, it is to know Him as the truth. It is this knowing that makes true faith different from all the false kinds of faith that are in the world.

Third, it is to have the whole Christ dwell in you by faith. It is Christ in the text, not Christ as justifying or dying only, but the whole of Him, for faith is capable of taking in the whole of Him, and He affects the heart accordingly. There is a parallel Scripture to this:

1. From *Exposition of Ephesians; Works* 2:411–12.

"When it pleased God to reveal his Son to me" (Gal. 1:16). For Christ the Son to reveal Himself to a man is for the whole of Him to dwell in the heart by faith. It is not only revealing Christ *to* me, but revealing Christ *in* me. Oh, it is a vain and wicked imagination that every man has an unrevealed Christ within him, and the work of salvation is revealing what is in the heart already. Rather, for Christ to be revealed in us is for Christ to be so revealed as to be in the midst of us; it is for Jesus Christ to dwell in the heart continually, so that we receive an abundance of Him; it is to have the image and representation of all He is; and it is to know by Him, in my heart—the whole Christ, not one piece of Him. Brethren, the whole of Christ, and not one piece of Him only, all His words and all His speeches, is Christ dwelling in you by faith; when you receive all of them, it is the whole Christ.

Fourth, it is all of Christ, all about Him. You read of a great many things of Christ, of His dying, His rising, how He walked, what He is to His people in His relations, in His dealings. If faith has Christ present with the soul and knows one thing, more and more of Christ, thereby Christ is said to dwell in the soul. So it is by letting Him into the soul and into the heart and affecting the heart with Him. The apostle says, "I am in travail with you till Christ be formed in you" (Gal. 4:19). He speaks here of the point of justification. Christ justifies by restoring their faith to see their justification in Christ again and drawing their hearts to seek it in Christ. This is Christ formed in them; for Christ as my justification to take my heart and possess my soul is for Christ, in and by that particular thing, to dwell in me. "If ye abide in me, and my words abide in you" (John 15:7a); abiding is dwelling. Let Him dwell and have a power upon my soul. This is for Christ to abide—every beam of Christ is Christ dwelling Himself, being present by faith to the soul.

Fifth, it is for Christ, and all of Christ, every beam of Him, not only to be known but to take and affect my heart. You see, the heart is made the subject of Christ's dwelling; it is not to dwell in the notion, in your brains. You have no indwelling of Christ unless your hearts are affected. This is expressly said: "We all, beholding with open face the glory of the Lord, are changed into the same image from glory to glory, by the Spirit of the Lord" (2 Cor. 3:18). First, there is spiritual beholding; he speaks of Christ, not only of His person, but of all that is to be known of Christ. Adam's graces had no glory, but all of Christ's do. Such a beholding, letting Christ and His glory into the soul, changes it, turns it, and leaves impressions on it. This is done by the Spirit of the Lord. By "the Spirit of the Lord" the apostle does not mean the Holy Ghost, for he said in the words before, "The Lord is that Spirit." It is Christ Himself, by His force and power when He comes into the soul, who changes it, fills it, quickens it, strengthens it, and leaves impressions on it. As the burning glass contracts all the beams of the sun to a point, but it is the beams of the sun that set on fire the cloth, so it is the Spirit of the Lord that fires our hearts. Thus, to know Christ is to dwell in Him.

William Ames (1576–1633)

Puritan at Cambridge, exiled to the Netherlands and known as the “Learned Doctor.” Ames's influence was still felt at Cambridge while Goodwin was there.

7

Christ's Perfections Are Our Perfections[1]

If you are true and right Christians, and you know, as the apostle says, how to put a due estimate on what is your greatest interest and privilege in this life—the proof and trial of your graces, and of the grace of patience above all, as the highest perfection of a Christian, yea, of Christ Himself, and the most eminent praise of prophets and apostles—and if you value being rendered most pleasing to God, then count it all joy when you fall into temptations. For now you have God and Christ, the great, the Chief Master Orderer and Designer of these conflicts, setting His most gracious eye on you, pleasing Himself to behold how valiantly, wisely, and gallantly you behave and acquit yourselves. He sits in heaven as the great Spectator of these jousts and tournaments, which are to Him as spectacles which are sports to us. The apostle alludes to this when he writes, "For I think that God hath set forth us the apostles last, as it were appointed to death: for we are made a spectacle unto the world, and to angels, and to men" (1 Cor. 4:9). Rejoice, therefore, just as good soldiers would rejoice to enter into battle in the sight of their great

1. From *Patience and its Perfect Work; Works* 2:434–35.

general and emperor, whom they have given themselves to please.

Thus, "No man that warreth entangleth himself with the affairs of this life, that he may please him who hath chosen him to be a soldier" (2 Tim. 2:4). Therefore, get your hearts free and loose from all those entanglements that arise from adherency to the things of this world; from inordinate passions that cleave to the things of this life, which hinder and weaken you from patiently bearing the losses and crosses you meet with in it. You cannot please the Captain of your salvation or approve yourselves more to Him than by a patient endurance, which is seen when Paul exhorts Timothy, "Therefore endure hardness as a good soldier of Christ" (v. 3). In the context of the next verse, it is as if he says, "it pleaseth your general to see it." In Colossians 1:10, he first prays in general terms, "that they might walk worthy of the Lord unto all pleasing." This pleasing consists in fruitfulness in good works, or the active life of a Christian. But in the next verse he speaks of being strengthened with all might to all patience and long-suffering, and this is the chiefest and most glorious part that a Christian is to perform—the part that consummates the other. Therefore, this part requires a more glorious power to work it than the former, the active part, did, as verse 11 shows, "Strengthened with all might, according to his glorious power, unto all patience and long-suffering."

8

Three Hours[1]

"He took on him the form of a servant" (Phil. 2:7). And He was such a servant as could not have been hired among all the creatures. They all could not do the work that He did: "The government of the whole world is upon his shoulders" (Isa. 9:6). He has relieved His Father of it for the present, but when He has brought Him infinite revenues of glory, He will at last "deliver up the kingdom to him" (1 Cor. 15:24) with a greater surplus than would have resulted from the course of providence taken up at the creation. And if you will not reckon that as a part of satisfaction, consider the service He did in the priest's office, wherein God acknowledged Him His servant.

He dispatched more work in those thirty-three years He lived, yea, in those three hours He suffered, than ever was or will be done by all creatures until eternity. It was a good six days of work when the world was made, and He had a principal hand in that; neither has He been idle since: "I and my Father work hitherto," says Christ (John 5:17). But that three hours' work on the cross was more than all the other. More will not be done in eternity than virtually was done in those three hours....

1. From *Christ the Mediator; Works* 5:102–103.

As they say that eternity is all time contracted into an instant, so all time, past and to come, was contracted into those few hours, as well as the merit of them. For He then made work for the Spirit, and indeed for all three persons, to eternity. He did that which the Spirit is writing out in grace and glory forever, and all that ever was or will be done toward the saints was then perfected: "He perfected for ever them that are sanctified, by that one offering" (Heb. 10:12, 14).

9

Christ by Piecemeal[1]

In Christ are treasures that will require digging to the end of the world. Men would be weary if they had the same light still, so God chooses to make known the same truth through new and diverse lights. Thus, God reveals Himself by piecemeal.... This may humble young Christians, who think, when they are first converted, that they have all knowledge, and therefore take it on themselves to censure men who have been long in Christ, and frame opinions out of their own experience, comparing few notes. Alas, you know but a little piece of what you shall know! When you have been in Christ ten or twenty years, then speak; then the opinions you have now will have fallen off and experience will have showed them to be false. They think themselves as Paul, that nothing can be added to them. But what does Paul say? "When I was a child"; he makes a comparison to a child, writing as a man who has been raised up to his spiritual estate. You also will "put away childish things" (1 Cor. 13:11).

If God in former ages revealed Himself by piecemeal, and if that piecemeal knowledge, which they had inch by inch, made them holy—for how holy were Enoch and Abraham, who had but one prom-

1. From *Three Sermons on Hebrews 1:1–2; Works* 5:529–30.

ise—then how much more holy should we be, having such a full revelation! If one promise wrought so much on their hearts, how much should so many promises on ours!

God works on men by degrees. Solomon makes the comparison that righteousness shines as the dawning of the day, until it comes to perfect day. Conversion out of the state of nature into the state of grace is called coming "out of darkness into light." Now light comes into the world by degrees. A man who sits up in the night cannot discern when the first break of day happens; it is half or a quarter of an hour afterward when he begins to see light. Thus it is with many poor souls; light breaks in upon them, so that they can tell that they were in darkness, but they do not know the instant when this light broke in, because God reveals Himself by degrees.

10

Christ, the Marrow of the Gospel[1]

This is the common use or corollary from both [of] what God has done and what fullness dwells in Christ: that sinners and enemies of God may obtain peace and reconciliation with Him. This, my brethren, is the marrow of the gospel; it is such good news that, as soon as it burst out, heaven and earth rang with joy again. The angels could not hold back, but, being ambitious to relate it, came down to earth to bring the first news of it: "Peace on earth, good-will towards men" (Luke 2:13, 14).

Though you can hear it and be no more moved than the seats you sit on, yet when it was first preached it brought in men as volunteer troops, more than the law had. The law and the prophets were till John: but since then the kingdom of God (that is, the gospel) is preached, and every man presseth into it (Luke 16:16). But now, alas, we who are used to the daily tidings of it are little moved with it! How few come in upon proclamation of it! Therefore, we are driven to make it our greatest business to preach the law, to come with that great hammer to break your bones in pieces first, that we then may preach the gospel (as in Isaiah 62) to the captives, and to bind up the broken-hearted, and so to make ourselves work;

1. From *Reconciliation by the Blood of Christ; Works* 5:512.

and this we count our misery. This we profess before you all this day, that we tremble most when we come to preach it, for we are afraid that men should go on lying in their sins. If they do so, they might as well have been in hell as in the church to hear it, because God may be provoked to swear against them that they shall never enter into His rest.

11

Reconciliation through Christ[1]

Our God is love, even love itself: "And we have known and believed the love God hath to us. God is love; and he that dwelleth in love dwelleth in God, and God in him" (1 John 4:16). God's love is infinite just as He Himself is, and He loves to show the utmost of His love. Of all works, works of love have the most delight in them; therefore, mercy is called His delight, His darling: "Who is a God like unto thee, that pardoneth iniquity, and passeth by the transgression of the remnant of his heritage?" (Micah 7:18). He does not retain His anger forever, because He delights in mercy. Thus, our God being love, and mercy being His delight, He would gladly show how well He can love creatures; He was most glad of the greatest opportunity to show it. Therefore, He resolves upon this course, to reconcile enemies, whatever the cost, for the more they should cost Him, the more glad they should be. The making of a thousand new friends could not have expressed so much love as the reconciling of one enemy. To love and delight in friends, who had never wronged Him, was too narrow, shallow, and slight a way. He had heights, depths, breadth of love. Who is "able to comprehend with all saints what is the breadth, and length, and

1. From *Christ the Mediator*, *Works* 5:13–14.

depth, and height" (Eph. 3:18)? He wanted to make known the heights and depths of His love, and nothing except the depths of our misery could have drawn them out.

This is the reason "God commendeth his love towards us, in that, while we were yet sinners, Christ died for us.... For if, when we were enemies, we were reconciled to God by the death of his Son, much more, being reconciled, we shall be saved by his life" (Rom. 5:8, 10). God commends His love toward us, that while we were His enemies, He gave His Son for us, not to be born only but to die. Both our being sinners and His giving of His Son commend or set out His love, and He chose this course so that He might commend it. And the fact that this love is poured out on men, not the angels who fell, further commends His love. There were only two kinds of sinners whose sins could be taken away; of the two, who would not have thought that the fallen angels would be addressed first and have passed more easily? They were fairer and better creatures than we, and if He regarded service, one of them was able to do more for Him than a thousand of us. Also, when He had bought us, He would face a great deal more trouble to preserve and care for us than we would ever be able to requite in service and attendance upon Him.

12

"Christ above Moses"[1]

"See that ye refuse not him that speaketh. For if they escaped not who refused him that spake on earth, much more shall not we escape, if we turn away from him that speaketh from heaven: whose voice then shook the earth: but now he hath promised, saying, Yet once more I shake not the earth only, but also heaven. And this word, Yet once more, signifieth the removing of those things that are shaken, as of things that are made, that those things which cannot be shaken may remain. Wherefore we receiving a kingdom which cannot be moved, let us have grace, whereby we may serve God acceptably with reverence and godly fear: for our God is a consuming fire."

—Hebrews 12:25–29

If God (whom the apostle here affirms Christ to be) will come down into the world a second time, He will surely make His revelation there exceed the former. It is His manner so to do, especially if the first is merely a shadow or type of the same person in lesser fullness (as Moses was a type of Christ) and is of the earth; then, the second or next succeeding, whatever it be, will rise as high as heaven in comparison to the former.

1. From *Supereminence of Christ*; *Works* 5:442.

Now Moses gave forth his dispensation as a man on earth, but Christ as the Lord from heaven; therefore, His must exceed Moses' in proportion. His argument runs thus: It was Christ's own voice that shook the earth when He gave the law. He was concealed under the administration of angels in His speaking to Moses (so He is sometimes termed an angel, sometimes the Lord [Acts 7:30–32]), and He also was disguised under Moses as he received the law, as His type. Yet if in this hiddenness He owned and seconded that dispensation so far as to shake the earth in testimony of that underhand and remote presence of His, what effects will His voice have when He appears personally and professedly as the Son of God to dwell in man's nature personally united to Himself, and therein to deliver a new doctrine (namely, the gospel)? And what effects might His voice have now, after His having been on earth and there having conversed with men, but now being ascended again to heaven, from whence He speaks and rules, who, in His person, was the Lord from heaven (1 Cor. 15), and in heaven while on earth, and so Lord of both earth and heaven, and has received all power both in earth and heaven? To give full proof of all these things, He will therefore surely shake both earth and heaven, and show He is able to shake and remove both.

13

God's Greatest Work (1)[1]

What was the greatest work of wonder God ever did in the world? It was the incarnation of the Son of God: "How long wilt thou go about, O thou backsliding daughter? for the LORD hath created a new thing in the earth, A woman shall compass a man" (Jer. 31:22). God has created (says the prophet) a new thing in the earth, namely, that a woman should encompass in her womb that *Gheber,* that strong and giant-like man, Christ, God and man, without the help of man. At the moment when this was done, there was a manifestation and declaration of all three persons in it. A record is extant how all, though invisibly, concurred in it, not darkly, with an "us" in general words, as at the creation, "Let us make man," but clearly and distinctly. As you find Moses, Christ, and Elijah talking and conferring together at the transfiguration of Christ (which Peter sees as the most solemn and most glorious manifestation of God to which he was an eye- and ear-witness, 2 Peter 1:16–17) to grace the solemnity of it, so here the very conference is recorded. It was a set and solemn conference in heaven, and the words spoken were set down at the instant of Christ's conception, the Father declaring His decree about it to the Son,

---

1. From *The Work of the Holy Ghost in our Salvation*; *Works* 6:418.

and the Son speaking to the Father of His willingness to do it.

Paul recorded and set down the very words as a great secret (as it must be accounted) in Hebrews 10:5: "When he comes into the world, he says...." It is the Son of God of whom he speaks, as existing before He took man's nature. The words that follow are expressly said to be spoken by Him at the time, instant, or moment of His coming into the world and being made flesh, as prophesied by David; Paul affirms He then uttered them. His taking of flesh was a going forth from His Father (as He Himself styles it in John), the setting out upon the greatest adventure and design that ever was.

14

God's Greatest Work (2)[1]

Therefore, Christ, at the time of His first setting forth, thought fit to speak something about it, as a distinct person from His Father and as He who should be interested in it (for none was to be made a sacrifice but He), to let Him know on what ground He undertook it—merely in obedience to His will. He did the same when He suffered: "Not my will, but thine be done," which was His motto from first to last. "Sacrifice and offering thou (as speaking to His Father) wouldest not, but a body hast thou prepared me" (Heb. 10:5).

As Christ is thus expressly introduced, it should be noted that His Father had given the occasion, having first declared to Him and revived the remembrance of His everlasting decrees and prophecies about it. For the speech of Christ, "Then said I, Lo I come to do thy will" (Heb. 10:7), is evidently in answer to another speech uttered and declared to Him by His Father, which He repeats in verse 6: "When in burnt offerings and sacrifices for sins, thou, Father, hadst had no pleasure, then or thereupon said I, Lo, I come...." These words also revive the memory of God's decree and an old record about it: "In the volume of the book it is written of me to do thy will,

1. From *The Work of the Holy Ghost in our Salvation*; *Works* 6:418–19.

God." God the Father has declared His will, and the Son His, and the Holy Ghost, the secretary of heaven, is brought in as a recorder of all this: "Whereof the Holy Ghost is a witness" (Heb. 10:15).

That word also bids us to accept this assertion of Christ, as that which is referred to, as well as to that quotation that followed. He was in a peculiar manner in this, for no one but He could have told it as uttered at that very time. For this Christ has expressly told us, that as He and His Father confer together about the great transactions of man's salvation, the Spirit hears all that They say (John 16:13). He did not stand by as a bare witness to relate it and confirm it to us, but was sent down by both as a principal actor, who had the great and ultimate hand in effecting it.

The Son of God speaks of a body prepared by the Father for Him to take up: "A body hast thou prepared me" (Heb. 10:5). The Father had a hand in it then, but by whom? By the Holy Ghost: "The Holy Ghost shall come upon thee, and the power of the Highest shall overshadow thee: therefore shall that holy thing that shall be born of thee be called the Son of God" (Luke 1:35). Here, then, we see, if not a visible theophany (as our divines call that appearance of the Spirit at His baptism), at least an evident record of an invisible and distinct conjunction of all three persons at the moment of Christ's conception, each having a part in it:

1. The Father declaring it as His will, both to the Son and the Spirit.

2. The Holy Ghost, as the person sent by the Father to perform and fashion that body in Mary's

womb; this tabernacle that God pitched, not man (Heb. 8:2; 9:11).

3. The Son, as the person who owns and assumes that body prepared for Him to dwell in it, as in a tabernacle, as the author to the Hebrews terms it: "Lo I come into the world," which He did only by taking that body to Himself, into one person with Him.

The Assertion of Liberty of Conscience by the Independents at the Westminster Assembly of Divines.

Goodwin, Philip Nye, Sidrach Simpson, William Bridge, and Jeremiah Burroughs became known as the "Dissenting Brethren" of the Assembly due to their independent or congregational theory of church government.

(Painted by John Rogers Herbert [1810–1890])

15

Possessing Christ by Faith[1]

A man does not possess Christ by faith in the way he possesses money in his cupboard or deeds of land, which he takes for granted that he has and yet perhaps never looks at once a year. No; Christ is as meat that a man feeds on, chews, and digests, and whose stomach works on continually. The man lives on Him every day; that is the application of faith (John 6:53). If other bread is our daily food, then surely Christ is much more; therefore it is called the life of faith: "The life I live is by the faith on the Son of God" (Gal. 2:20). Life is a continuation of action and motion; as the heart is the principle of life—it always beats, and if it lies still a man dies—such is faith. Faith is not a sleeping thing, nor merely not doubting that Christ is mine, but a continual active whetting of my thoughts on Christ as mine, or casting myself upon Him to be mine. It is living on Him and in Him.

Some men live in a good opinion of themselves and are confident that Christ is theirs; they are not sued or troubled in this confidence by Satan's temptations, and no doubts come to put them out of a sense of possession. This they account to be faith and take for granted that they shall never be cast out.

---

1. From *The Object and Acts of Justifying Faith*; *Works* 8:331–32.

In practice, many understand faith to be belief and persuasion only, so they make faith a good persuasion and opinion of their present condition. The object and goal of their faith is their own estate, and not Christ and His love, so their faith is not a good opinion of Him or founded on the daily thoughts they have of His merit, satisfaction, mercy, grace, righteousness, etc. Their faith is a good opinion of themselves, arising out of the self-flattery of their own hearts, so that they honor not Christ in their thoughts so much as themselves; theirs is a judgment of charity to themselves rather than faith in Christ. I call it that charitable opinion that one Christian is bound to have of others, the assumption that they are the children of God, that their eternal state is good, and that they are in Christ. Such a charitable opinion of themselves, whereby, as the apostle says of the Hebrews, they are persuaded of good things concerning themselves, is the only faith of a great many people; but this is not to believe on Christ, but on themselves. The fact that their own estate is indeed the object of their faith is evident by this, that if any man goes about to discover his natural condition while he is without true faith, he soon becomes upset, and says, "You would bring me to unbelief and despair." This is because an apprehension that his present state is good is that, and all that, which he reckons as faith. But those who seek his good would bring him from a false belief about his state and himself to a good and a true belief in Christ, and on God's free grace, which are the prime objects of faith.

16

One Foot on Christ, Another on Yourself?[1]

A common error in the faith of Protestants is that, though they put some trust and confidence in Christ, and in their opinions and sayings profess that they renounce all but Christ, yet secretly their own righteousness is the ground even of their very trust on Christ, and so they make themselves the rock of their trust on that only true rock—Christ. Thus, they think that Christ will save them for the smallness of their sins and good dispositions, and so in that respect they are nearer to Christ than others. The young man who came to Christ came indeed, but he was encouraged by having kept the commandments from his youth. These men stand as it were on two boughs, one of which is rotten, and so must fall and perish. One foot they have on Christ, but another on themselves, on their own good works, and even though they trust not in these works under the notion of merit (as the papists hold), yet in a lower way they trust in them, as that which their souls in their confidence put their weight most upon, and as that which commends them to God and makes them acceptable to Him. So

1. From *The Object and Acts of Justifying Faith*; *Works* 8:332.

they trust not completely on the grace revealed by Christ (1 Peter 1:13).

These use Christ and His righteousness as many ministers seeking pulpits use the king's title. They procure his title to strengthen their own titles, which they have from their patrons, but they do not rely chiefly on the king's; they acquire it merely to make everything sure. Such is the case of these men; their souls have secret recourse to their own goodness more than to Christ, although in the meantime they are sound in their opinions about justification by faith and by Christ only.

17

No Union, No Justification[1]

Because all acts of God's justification of us depend on union with Christ, on our having Him and being in Him, and thereby having a right to His righteousness, therefore, it should be the aim of a soul casting itself on Christ to have justification from Him also to have union with Him; it may and ought to cast itself on God and Christ, to be made one with Him. There is as much a reason and occasion for such an act as for the former, for union with Him is as much a privilege to be obtained as justification. For though we were one in Christ before God in representation from all eternity, and when He was on the cross, and by a covenant secretly made between God and Him, yet there is an actual implanting and engrafting into Christ that we obtain upon believing, and not till then, which the apostle calls baptizing, planting into Christ, and being in Christ (Rom. 6:2; 2 Cor. 5:17, Gal. 3:27). Until they receive this engrafting, even those who are elect are said to be "without Christ in the world" (Eph. 2:12).

So a man may and ought at first to look at Christ as yet to be obtained, and so seek after that union with Him that is yet to be wrought—union upon which this justification that is yet to be attained depends.

1. From *The Object and Acts of Justifying Faith*; *Works* 8:406

Paul says, "We accounted all loss, that we might win Christ, and obtain an interest and a share in him" (Phil. 3:8); so if there is both a union with Christ and a justification that depends on that union yet to be obtained, there is a just ground and occasion for a man to cast himself on Christ to obtain them. This casting, out of spiritual apprehensions and affections, is the very act that both makes this union and brings us into a state of justification; therefore, seeing Christ and coming to Him are the acts of justifying faith (John 6:35, 40).

18

Communion with Christ[1]

To sit down with Abraham, Isaac, and Jacob was the phraseology of the Old Testament (though Christ used it when He came at the close of that testament). But to sit down with the *us*, the three, another manner of three than Abraham, Isaac, and Jacob; to sit down with God the Father, God the Son, and God the Holy Ghost, and to have Them dwell in us, and to dwell in Them—this is Christ's language; this is New Testament language. Oh, to be bound up in that bundle of life with the living God and with Christ, who has life in Himself! Oh, let this be the whole strength of the aim of our souls, and let us be so moved and affected with it, so as not to lack a part and share in and with this good company! They were sufficient company to Themselves when They inhabited eternity, and They are sufficient to make us so, by taking us up into Their intimate converse.

Suppose God had chosen only one soul besides that man Jesus, whom He took up into one person with His Son (for we mere creatures could not have been immediately united to God without a Mediator of union who was more than a creature; therefore, His presence is necessary for our happiness, as we

1. From *Election*; *Works* 9:149.

see in verse 24). How infinitely blessed that one soul would have been in the sole and single society of God the Father, Son, and Holy Ghost, and with the man Jesus, made one person with the Son; he would not have needed to have had the company of Peter and Paul to have made his happiness perfect, but “I in thee, and thou in me” would have made that soul perfect in one. The happiness that the saints have from their oneness with one another is only an additional and derived happiness; but “I in them, and thou in me, that they may be made perfect in one” makes their happiness solid, and gives it its substance. If Christ had said of that single soul, “Father, I will that this soul also whom thou hast given me, may be with me where I am, that it may behold my glory which thou hast given me,” this soul would have been perfectly happy. Have any of you had experience at any time—I do not say of grace, if you have not had it—of “My Father will love him, and I will love him, and will manifest myself to him” (John 14:21); that is, have you had the Father tell you that He loves you? Then again, have you had the Son say to your poor souls how He loves you, and manifests Himself and His heart to you? And have you had the Holy Ghost communicate Himself in like manner; and this vouchsafed in this life in some short converses of each of these persons with your souls, which are but imperfect manifestations of them to us in this life?

Oh, what sweetness will there be one day in heaven in the fullness of converse and manifestation of these three persons. It will be, if not all, yet the great discourse that will be had and heard in heaven with your poor souls by the three persons, bringing all the delights They have had in you from eternity down into your hearts, and revealing Them to you to all eternity.

Oliver Cromwell (1599–1658)

Lord Protector of England from 1653–1658. Goodwin became an advisor to Cromwell, and a principle architect of the church under the Cromwell era.

19

Elected to Inseparable Union with Christ[1]

Imagine that a great, lofty, and spirited prince, one who is Lord of all, should deign to take the lowest beggar into his care and bestow his son or prince upon her in marriage, thereby uniting himself with her in the nearest tie and bond of union. Earthly kings are kings only by birth, and in their essence or nature they are of the same kind as other men, and yet God does this. To conclude this, in Romans 8:39 you read that "neither height, nor depth,... shall be able to separate us from the love of God, which is in Christ Jesus our Lord." *Shall not separate* implies a union made; *heights* are those heights of God's loftiness, in being so infinitely above us; the *depths* are your depths of lowness, miseries, and sins.

Now these depths did not hinder His conjunction with us at first, nor shall they ever separate or turn away His heart from us. In marriages of people who are of lowly birth (though perhaps rich) with or into the nobility, it often happens that the height and loftiness of the noble spouses makes them in time despise those they have married, so that their hearts are turned away from them because of the dispropor-

1. From *Election*; *Works* 9:118.

tion in respect to class, so that such marriages prove to be uncomfortable unions in the long run. But it is not thus with the lofty heart of our God. His loftiness and your lowness, His heights and your depths, make the happiest union ever, because it is His grace that makes it and brings it about, and holds us together.

20

Purchasing and Bestowing[1]

By His death, Christ purchased all of the grace and glory that the God of all grace had designed for us. That is clear from Scripture: "For by one offering he hath perfected for ever them that are sanctified" (Heb. 9:14). Alas for us poor creatures! For a long time after we are sanctified, we remain imperfect, lacking all and everything in comparison. How, then, are we perfected? Because Jesus Christ, by that one offering, perfectly purchased all that ever shall go to make up our perfection. It is finished in that sense. He so abundantly procured all by His death that He needed to offer Himself but once. If there were anything necessary to perfect a saint that Christ did not purchase, His offering must have been imperfect.

Likewise, when He first ascended into heaven, He as a head received every whit, the whole of all that should be given to us by the Spirit from God, even to all the saints that were then unborn; He received all of it all at once, though it shall be given forth to us by parcels to all eternity: "Therefore being by the right hand of God exalted, and having received of the Father the promise of the Holy Ghost, he hath shed forth this which ye now see and hear" (Acts 2:33).

---

1. From *Election*; *Works* 9:358.

By the intention of those acts, you easily may understand the intention of Christ's apprehension of us when He began actually applying to us that which He died for and received upon His ascension. At our calling, which is the beginning of the application of our salvation, Christ actually begins to apprehend us, which He has never done before, nor is said to have done before our calling.... He then takes hold of a soul for which He purchased all and received all, so as actually to give it to that soul. But although He begins from that time, what Christ first works in calling is not all or the whole for which He apprehended that soul; no, Christ merely begins with him, but He will not finish with him soon, but will continue the work to all eternity.

21

Gathered to Christ or Satan?[1]

Make sure to be one of this great assembly; let men flock to and get into Christ by clusters: "To him shall the gathering of the people be" (Gen. 49:10). Jesus Christ sets up His standard, which proclaims, "Come into Jesus Christ and be not as Judas, who fell short by iniquity from this lot." It is a fatal saying of Peter to Simon Magus, "Thou hast no part nor portion in this matter"; it is tragic that so innumerable a company should be gathered under this one Head but that you should be shut out.

To move you to it, I have two things out of the text: you must be gathered one way, either to Christ or Satan; you must fall either to Christ's or the devil's allotment and share. As Christ is the Head of all that shall be saved (Eph. 1:22), so the devil is the head of all the children of disobedience (Eph. 2:2). And as Christ is the Head of the angels, though He is not of the same nature with them, so is the devil of men.

At the end of the world, when Christ shall have taken out all of His own, all the rest shall be cast into the fire prepared for the devil and his angels. The expression in the Old Testament was that men were "gathered to their fathers," but the wicked were gathered unto *coetus gigantum*—that is, "the company of

1. From *Ephesians*; *Works* 1:198.

the giants," those wicked ones before the flood, from whom hell has its denomination, as the first inhabitants of it (Prov. 21:16). So the language of the New Testament is "gathered to the devil and his angels," to the fire prepared for them.

22

Sitting at the Right Hand[1]

Some would restrain the exaltation of Christ's sitting at God's right hand only to the human nature. They say that as He was the Son of God simply considered, He always sat at God's right hand. But the mistake lies in this: It is true that, as the Son of God, He has had an equal power with the Father from everlasting, but that power is never expressed by sitting at God's right hand, for then the Holy Ghost should be said to sit at God's right hand as well as God the Son, which is never said. But Christ's sitting at God's right hand implies the power that is committed to Him as Mediator, both God and man; that is, as He is the Son of God, clothed with man's nature and exalted now in heaven.

Thus, what is attributed to the one is attributed to the other by communication of properties. We say that God and man died, though the manhood only died; it is attributed to the whole, it is called the "blood of God." We say that the God-man rose, though only His body rose; it is attributed to the whole, *totus Christus,* though not *totum Christi.*[2] The whole Christ

1. From *Ephesians*; *Works* 1:476–77.

2. *Totus/totum,* a commonly used distinction by Reformed theologians, refers to the omnipresence of Christ. Richard Muller says, "The

rose and the whole Christ sits at God's right hand; He exalted Him, though not the whole of Christ.

---

totus Christus, i.e., the whole person of Christ, is omnipresent, inasmuch as the divine person is, by virtue of his divinity, omnipresent; but the *totum Christi,* all of Christ, i.e., both natures, cannot be omnipresent, since the human nature must be in one place" (*Dictionary of Latin and Greek Theological Terms* [Grand Rapids: Baker, 1985], 305).

23

Summed Up in Christ[1]

> "That in the dispensation of the fulness of times he might gather together in one all things in Christ, both which are in heaven, and which are on earth; even in him."
>
> — Ephesians 1:10

God, intending to sum up all things in heaven and in earth in Christ, first sums up all things in heaven and in earth in Christ's person, as the foundation of the summing up of a mystical body, too. God summed up all sorts of divisions in Christ.

First, He cast God and the creature up into one sum, for He made God and the creature one Person. In the second place, whereas He had two reasonable creatures, angels and men, He takes the nature of a man and unites it to God and the condition of an angel, for that is His due, too. That man (if He is united to God) is called "the heavenly man"; He is not an earthly man, nor to be an earthly man, though for our sins He took frail flesh; but it is His due to be a man and like an angel for condition. He sums up the condition of things in heaven, and the nature of men on earth, in His own person.

Then come down to earth, and there you have Jew and Gentile; He summed up both in Christ, for

1. From *Ephesians*; *Works* 1:170, 173.

Christ came of both. Jew and Gentile, all the world, Christ and all, had the very same great-grandfathers, those ten men that were from Adam to Noah. Thus, He summed up all in His person. When He had done, He summed up of all a body answerable to His person, a church, a city of the living God, a family to Him, as Scripture expresses it. He takes of all things in heaven and of all things in earth, and He makes them up to Christ as a Head, one body.

Therefore, my brethren, long for this day, and let your hearts seek to be one of this number, not to be left out of this *all*. For your encouragement, consider this, which is a second observation: no condition can be said to be any hindrance to you from being in Christ.

You can raise no objections against yourself, neither poverty, nor folly, nor lack of memory and understanding, nor weakness, nor sinfulness; I say there is no objection at all that you can raise against yourself that may hinder your salvation. Why? Because God takes all sorts of things on earth. You can say nothing of yourself except that there are some whom God has saved who are just like you. "There is no difference," He says (Rom. 3:22); He "justifieth freely by his grace." There is no difference; a beggar and a king have the same shadow in the sun. Sins, my brethren, make no difference, either the greatness or the smallness of them, to hinder salvation.

24

Christ Putting Beauty on the Body[1]

"It is sown in dishonour; it is raised in glory."
—1 Corinthians 15:43a

The excellency of Adam's animal state of body was of beauty. He had a native beauty, as I may call it, an inbred beauty; he needed no clothes or any such thing to set it out. In that respect you find that though they were naked and had nothing to adorn them, yet they were in a glory, for when they had sinned, they fell to shame by reason of their nakedness. Adam had a beautiful body and so had Eve; it is said God built the woman. But all the beauty that Adam's body had was but a shadow of the beauty and glory that Christ will put on the bodies of His saints at the latter day, on the spiritual bodies mentioned here in the text.

We nowhere read that the beauty of Adam is called glory, but here we find the beauty of the saints called glory. Mark the expression in 1 Corinthians 15:43a: "It is sown in dishonour [namely, the body]; it is raised in glory." The word *glory* here has a special relation to that beauty, that excess of beauty, that God will put on the bodies of the saints in heaven. You must know this, that in Scripture the excess of any excellency is called glory. We say that fire has a

1. From *Creatures and their Condition in Creation*; *Works* 7:121–23.

light in it, but we do not call fire glorious; but because the sun has an excess of light in it, we call the sun glorious.

Yes, my brethren, it is most certain that the bodies of the saints shall so shine as to put down or eclipse the glory of the sun. As a candle waxes pale in the presence of the sun, or as the fire is put out by the sun shining on it in the summer, so shall the bodies of the saints do. Isaiah 24:23 says, "Then the moon shall be confounded, and the sun shall be ashamed, just as you see a candle looks pale, or as the fire draws in its own beams of light before the sun, when the Lord of hosts shall reign in mount Zion, and in Jerusalem, and before his ancients gloriously." Although this passage may not be referring to the complete fulfillment of the glory of the saints at the latter day, it is an allusion to it. The sun and moon shall be ashamed and confounded, and as a candle now appears before the sun, so shall the sun appear before that glory that shall be put on the body of Christ and the bodies of the saints.

25

Living Like Christ[1]

As the kingdom of Jesus Christ is not of this world, neither is the majesty of His kingdom. Therefore, it is not the heaping up of riches, learning, worldly respect, and authority that advances this majesty, but endeavoring to be holy as God is holy (1 Peter 1:15). It is by holy living, by living as Christ would if He were here. It is to be merciful as He is merciful; kind, faithful, and true as He is; pardoning injuries as He does; and purifying yourselves as He is pure. In a word (as you have it in 1 John 4:17), it is demeaning yourselves here as God would if He were in the world.

Therefore, do not think you cannot advance the majesty of the Lord because of your poor outward condition; that is, because you are poor, condemned, despised, and not regarded in the world. For Christ was all these, and yet the majesty of the Lord appeared in Him, of which Peter says they were eyewitnesses (2 Peter 1:16). In all these conditions, you may approve yourself to the consciences of men, as Christ did. You may be poor, but if you keep your sincerity and do not use deceitful, base, and unlawful means, but walk faithfully in your calling, manifest that you live by faith and depend on God, and show a contentment in your condition, and that you live a

1. From *Gospel Holiness*; *Works* 7:284.

more comfortable life by the help of faith, delighting yourself in the Almighty, than those that have the most abundance, the majesty of the Lord will appear more in you than in a professor who glisters more in the world with regard to outward things.

26

The Revenues of His Death[1]

Consider the meritorious cause of [heaven], which is Christ the Lord of glory. Christ Jesus Himself has purchased it for us in His blood, He has laid the foundation of it, His blood was laid out for it; He spun this thread of glory out of His own bowels. Therefore, we may well argue the greatness of this glory, seeing that His blood has obtained it (Eph. 1:18). It is there called "the riches of the glory of his inheritance." Christ distributes all the inheritance that He has to the saints. This is said to be a purchased possession; my brethren, think with yourselves: What shall be the revenues of glory purchased by His death? Think what a large possession the blood of Christ will procure. Consider with yourselves what this will amount to. This is heaven; heaven is the revenues of Christ's blood. Think, I say, what a glorious heaven it must be that Christ's blood has purchased for us. This is what He aimed to do in laying down His life for us; for justification, adoption, and sanctification are but the way to glorification; we are justified, adopted, and sanctified to this end, that we might be glorified.

Consider, therefore, what Christ's blood will be worth, what the revenues of it will come to; and therefore let what has been said of heaven move you

1. From *The Blessed State of Glory*; *Works* 7:460.

and work on you. If I should single out any man present, any particular man in this congregation, as our Savior did the young man in the gospel, and bid him forsake all so that he might have treasure in heaven, this would be a great offer. Now I single out every man here; consider with yourselves that you all stand arrested before God, for you deserved to be accursed eternally, yet if you leave all your iniquities, repent, and believe, you shall have glory in heaven. I think you should take hold of this offer and regard no strictness as too much, that you might get heaven. If you were good businessmen, you would not let heaven, this precious heaven, pass you; you would lay hold of it and spend all you had to get it, that you might be made partakers of those invaluable treasures.

Think within yourself—you cannot bid enough for it. First Corinthians 9:25 says, "Strive and run, so run that you may attain; and every one that striveth for the mastery is temperate in all things. Now they do it that they may have a corruptible, but we an incorruptible, crown." If men are so careful here on earth to obtain temporal preferments, much more, then, we should run to get that preferment that is the chief, even everlasting happiness in heaven. It is heaven, an incorruptible crown, that transcends all other things.

And think with yourselves how it will trouble you if you come short of your prize! What a fearful and sorrowful cry will be yours—who will express your anguish?—when you hear that heaven and your crown are parted from you! It was a pitiful saying to Nebuchadnezzar, "Thy kingdom is departed from thee"; it will be much more pitiful to any of us to hear that we have lost heaven. How it will astonish you to hear Christ say, "Heaven and thy crown is departed from you, you must be turned to devils for ever, for this will be your condition to eternity!"

John Owen (1616–1683)

Puritan at Oxford, called the "prince of English divines." Owen and Goodwin served as advisors to Oliver Cromwell and were leading voices for Congregationalism.

27

Joy in God's Glory[1]

We shall be made one with Him; these are Christ's own words: "That they all may be one; as thou, Father, art in me, and I in thee, even that they be also one in us: that the world may believe that thou hast sent me. And the glory that thou gavest me I have given them; that they may be one, as we are one: I in them, and thou in me, that they may be made perfect in one; and that the world may know that thou hast sent me, and hast loved them, as thou hast loved me" (John 17:21–23).

My brethren, what is it that makes God happy but God Himself? And what is it that makes Christ so happy but that He is equal with God the Father? Now, if God makes Himself happy, how happy shall we be when we communicate with God in His happiness? To be one with Him, then, must make us happy. We cannot be one with Him as Christ is, for He is the brightness of His glory, the express image and character of His person; He is the natural Son of God and of the same nature with God. But we shall be made one with Him so far as the creature is capable of being made one with Him, and we shall have the next union to that which God and Christ have with one another. Being made one with God, we shall

1. From *The Blessed State of Glory*; *Works* 7:463–64.

rejoice in all that God rejoices in. God's glory shall make you glorious, and you shall have all those joys by revenues out of His life in heaven. You shall rejoice more in God's happiness than in your own; the more happiness rises to God, the more happiness rises within you. That which is the substance of God's glory will be the substance of ours. It is the nature of love, that it rejoices in the love of the person beloved: "Ye are my friends, if ye do whatsoever I command you" (John 15:14).

Our Savior also said to His disciples, "If ye loved me, ye would have rejoiced, because I said I go to the Father." Now, my brethren, if we shall rejoice in the same things God rejoices in, both in that joy that is intrinsic within Him and in that joy that is extrinsic, by which He delights in all His works and providence; if both of these shall be in us, how glorious shall we be! In John 15:11, Christ says, "These things have I spoken unto you, that my joy might remain in you, and that your joy might be full." This is not to be understood of our Savior's joy of the hopes He had of them, but the joy that is in Christ shall be in us: "that my joy," He says, "may be in you." We shall enter into our Master's joy (Matt. 25:23) and rejoice in the hope of the glory of God. Not only so, but we rejoice also in God through our Lord Jesus Christ (Rom. 5:2). We shall rejoice not only in a created glory, which He shall bestow on us, but in God's own glory.

28

Weak, But Accepted for Christ's Sake[1]

Discouragement is the weakness of men's prayers. Though a man thinks his person is accepted, yet, "Alas," says he, "my prayers are so poor and weak, surely God will never regard them."

To remove this discouragement, let me first ask you this question: Do you pray with all your might? Then even though your strength is weak in itself and in your own estimation of it, yet because it is all the strength that you have, and because grace is in you, it shall be accepted. "For God accepts according to what a man hath, and not according to that he hath not" (2 Cor. 8:12).

You are to consider that God does not hear you for your prayers' sake (though not without them), but for His name's sake and His Son's sake, and because you are His child. The mother does not neglect to hear and relieve her child when the child cries, but she is tender, not because the child cries more loudly, but because the child cries, and the weaker the child is, the more pity she shows.

Again, though the performance in itself might be weak, yet considered as a prayer, it might be strong,

1. From *The Return of Prayers*; *Works* 3:399–400.

because a weak prayer may set the strong God to work. The faith we produce may be weak, yet because its object is Christ, therefore it justifies. So it is in prayer; it prevails, not because of the performance itself, but because of the name in which it is made, even Christ's name. Therefore, as a weak faith justifies, so a weak prayer prevails as well as a stronger, and both for the same reason, for faith attributes all to God, and so does prayer. As faith is merely a receiving grace, so prayer is a begging grace. Therefore, do you think your prayers are accepted at all, notwithstanding their weakness? If they are accepted, then they must be accepted as true prayers, and if they are accepted as prayers, then they must be accepted as effectual motives to prevail with God to grant the thing you ask; for if He should not accept them to that end for which they were ordained, it would be as if He did not accept them at all. Therefore, when He approves of any man's faith as true and sincere, He approves and accepts it to that purpose for which it was ordained, which is to save and justify, and to this end He just as fully accepts the weakest act of faith as the strongest. So it is with prayers, which, being ordained as a means to obtain mercies from Him, if He accepts them at all, it is with relation to the accomplishment of them, which is their end.

29

Christ's Works of Glory[1]

> "Saying with a loud voice, Worthy is the Lamb that was slain to receive power, and riches, and wisdom, and strength, and honour, and glory, and blessing."
>
> —Revelation 5:12

Glory is personally due to each person of the Godhead, but still each is proclaimed worthy to receive it on the occasion of some special work; so it is with Christ here.

The angels say of God the Father, "Blessing, and glory, and wisdom, and thanksgiving, and honour, and power, and might, be unto our God for ever and ever, Amen" (Rev. 7:12). All these are His due as God, and yet, in 4:11, He is proclaimed "worthy" to receive glory, honor, and such is the case for He "has created all things." So it is with Christ for having performed the work of redemption.

It is true that a glory is given to Christ that wholly relates to the work of redemption alone; even as to God the Father also, for and upon His work of creation. Although He was God and so almighty as to be able to create, yet He could not have had the glory of creating or being a Creator unless He had actually created. And so Christ has this glory given on the

1. From *A Discourse of Christ's Reward*; *Works* 3:220–21.

occasion of His being a Redeemer, and that He is a Redeemer; for He was slain, and without that He would not have been a Redeemer. Yet just as God, in and on the work of creation, receives only the glory of being God (the invisible things of God being manifested therein, even His eternal power and Godhead), so Christ, in receiving the glory of redemption, receives only the acknowledgments of those portions due to Him as the God-man, being now further manifested in that work.

30

Restoring Beauty to His Bride[1]

Let us suppose, in the manner of some romances, that a king was betrothed to a beautiful wife, whose picture was sent to him before he himself saw her. But when she set out on her journey to him, she fell sick of some loathsome disease, such as the smallpox or leprosy. But suppose that he knew before she came to him that she should be restored to her first primitive beauty, and that even though he knew he would be troubled by her disaster, distemper, or disease, he easily quieted himself for that little space of time in which her infirmity, though greatly disfiguring her, was to continue. For he himself would be her physician, the only one who could cure her and restore her to her first perfect beauty, which he knew he could and should do. Thus, he would show all love and peace toward her, even though her disease was loathsome, in full hope of her recovery.

This is the case between Christ and the church: "Husbands, love your wives, as Christ also loved the church: he that loveth his wife, loveth himself; for no man yet hated his own flesh, but nourisheth it, and cherisheth it, even as the Lord the church" (Eph. 5:25). If a man's flesh should be infected with the worst and foulest of diseases, even though he hates

1. From *Election*; *Works* 9:326.

the disease, yet he loves his own flesh and seeks out the cure for it; he nourishes his flesh and cherishes it. Christ does this also for those who are His flesh, the members of His body (v. 30). They are of His flesh and of His bone, much more than a man and wife are, they to whom this exhortation is directed (vv. 31–33). Therefore, Jesus Christ is so far from hating us, who are His own flesh, that He applies all sorts of remedies with a strong patience for the cure of our infirmities, and He is moved to do it with the greater patience because He knows we shall be restored to perfect health and soundness indeed, and He Himself shall be the healer. Finally, with an infinite love and joy, and glory to Himself, He will present us to Himself most glorious, without spot, wrinkle, or any such thing.

To conclude, I may say of this argument what the apostle says: "Beloved, now we are the sons of God, and it doth not yet appear what we shall be; but we know that when he shall appear, we shall be like him" (1 John 3:2). Does the apostle not say this to reassure you in the face of your unlikeness to God and Christ in this world? And do not God and Christ satisfy Themselves and satisfy Their hearts toward you in the midst of all your complaints of and about yourselves? I say of this, even as they do, that God has called you into glory; and though it does not appear to us what we shall be, nor what we are in regards to our title to this glory (for we are full of contrary, hateful iniquities), yet it appears to Christ what you are and shall be. And the time is coming when He shall present you glorious, without fault. If, as John says to them, "we know," then we can be sure God and Christ know this much more.

31

"The Son's Special Act"[1]

It was the Holy Ghost who formed Christ's human nature in the womb: Matthew 1:18 says, "Mary was found with child of the Holy Ghost," and verse 20 says, "That which is conceived in her is of the Holy Ghost." So He made the man Jesus, both body and soul.

Some divines further ascribe to the Spirit the special honor of tying that marriage knot, or union, between the Son of God and that man Jesus, whom He formed in the virgin's womb. If they mean that He, in common with the Father and the Son, joined in that great action, I grant it according to the measure of that general rule, *opera ad extra sunt indivisa* (the external works of the Trinity are undivided), which holds that all three persons have a common hand in all external works, or those that are not wrought within the Godhead itself, though there are some exceptions. But my subject is the special honor that belongs by way of eminency to the Holy Ghost in any of these works. After consideration, I have not found a ground to attribute the personal union more particularly to the Holy Ghost. Rather (according to my observation in the Scriptures and to consonant reason), that action is more peculiarly to be attributed

1. From *The Work of the Holy Ghost in our Salvation*; *Works* 6:11.

to the Son Himself, the second person, who took up into one person with Himself a human nature.

The Father indeed sent the Son into the world, to take flesh, and the Holy Ghost formed the flesh that He assumed, but it was the Son's special act to take it up into Himself and to assume it. So the apostle tells us in Hebrews 2:16 that He took on Him the seed of Abraham, or He took to Himself the very act of that union of His natures. It was His own single act, and rationally, it must have been so, for it was an act of a person knowing what He did when He did it. He took to Himself a foreign nature, to be one person with Himself, as a person affording His own subsistence unto that nature, to be a person with Himself. He Himself had to communicate that personality; no one else could do it for Him, for it was properly His own to bestow. Chapter 10 accords with this: "When he cometh into the world, he saith, 'A body hast thou prepared me'" (v. 5), speaking to His Father, who prepared that body by the Holy Ghost. It was His Father's ordination that He should take it, but He, existing before He took it and coming into the world by assuming it, says, "Lo, I come to do thy will, O God" (v. 7), stating it more expressly.

32

Spirit-Christology[1]

The Holy Ghost had the honor of consecrating Jesus to be the Christ by anointing Him "without" or "above measure," as John the Baptist witnessed (John 3:34). He was anointed with power and all grace: "The Spirit of the Lord shall rest upon him, and the Spirit of wisdom and understanding, the Spirit of counsel and might, the Spirit of knowledge and of the fear of the Lord" (Isa. 40:2). What is Messiah, or Christ, but the Most Holy One anointed (Dan. 9:24)? Now, with what oil was Jesus anointed and so made Christ? "God anointed Jesus of Nazareth with the Holy Ghost" (Acts 10:38). The Holy Ghost was that oil with which He was anointed above His fellows. He has His name of "Christ," which is the chief name of His person, from the Holy Ghost, as He has that of "Jesus" for saving us, which is His work. Christ, the anointed, is the name that speaks of all His offices. Kings, priests, and prophets, who were only His shadows, were anointed. It was the true and proper sign and token of His person being the Son of God that the Holy Ghost came visibly on Him and abode on Him: "And John bare record, saying, I saw the Spirit descending from heaven like a dove, and it abode upon him. And I knew him not: but he that

1. From *The Work of the Holy Ghost in our Salvation*; *Works* 6:11–13.

sent me to baptize with water, the same said unto me, upon whom thou shalt see the Spirit descending, and remaining on him, the same is he which baptizeth with the Holy Ghost. And I saw, and bare record, that this is the Son of God" (John 1:32–34). Compare that to John 7:38–39: "He that believeth on me, as the scripture hath said, out of his belly shall flow rivers of living water. (But this spake he of the Spirit, which they that believe on him should receive: for the Holy Ghost was not yet given; because that Jesus was not yet glorified)." Then note verses 40–41: "Many of the people, when they heard that saying, Of a truth, said they, this is that Prophet; others, This is the Christ."

This visible descending of the Spirit (which happened first to Him) was the highest possible confirmation of Jesus' identity as God's Son, except those words of the Father: "This is my beloved Son." The Baptist singles out two chief pieces of evidence, that He was baptized with the Holy Ghost as with fire and that He received the Spirit without measure (even though He was personally full of grace and truth, as He was the Son of God).

The Holy Ghost anointed Him to all His offices. He was anointed first to be a prophet and preacher of the gospel, which was first spoken by the Lord (Heb. 2:3). Thus, Luke 4:18 says (and some think it was His first text), "The Spirit of the Lord is upon me, because he hath sent me to heal the broken-hearted, to preach deliverance to the captives, and recovering of sight to the blind, to set at liberty them that are bruised."

Whether the Spirit was on Him as He preached or He was fitted to be a preacher because the Spirit was on Him makes no difference to my purpose. The Spirit made Him a preacher of the gospel, to utter things that no man ever did and to speak in such a manner as no man ever did. This is evident by the context in Luke 4, where He gave His first sermon after His baptism. The Holy Ghost had fallen on Him anew and He had returned full of the Holy Ghost (Luke 4:1). Likewise, in verse 14, He returned (or went) full of the Holy Ghost into Galilee, His standing diocese for His ordinary preaching, as the evangelists show.

The Holy Ghost anointed Him with power to do all His miracles and all His good works. He was anointed "with the Holy Ghost and with power... [and] went about doing good, and healing all that were oppressed of the devil" (Acts 10:38). It is expressly said that He cast out the devil by the Spirit (Matt. 12:28).

When Christ was dead, who raised Him up from the grave? This was such a great work that God Himself accounts it a new begetting, a second conception of Him, as it were, a new edition of His Son Christ: "He raised up Jesus again" (Acts 13:33). As it is written in the Psalms, "Thou art my Son, this day have I begotten thee." God rejoiced as if He had recovered and found His Son, who had been lost, as it were, in the likeness of sinful flesh. Who was the immediate cause of this new advancement, whereby He was born into the other world? The Holy Ghost: "But if the Spirit of him that raised up Jesus from the dead dwell in you, he that raised up Christ from the dead shall also quicken your mortal bodies, by his Spirit that dwelleth in you" (Rom. 8:11). God, by His Spirit, raises up both Christ and us.

When He ascended, who filled Him with glory? The Holy Ghost: He was "anointed with the oil of gladness above his fellows" (Ps. 45); this oil is said to be the Holy Ghost (Acts 10:33).

It was the Holy Ghost who solemnly anointed Him as King in heaven: "Being at the right hand of God, and having received of the Father the promise of the Holy Ghost" (Acts 2:33). From this Peter infers, "Therefore let all the house of Israel know assuredly, that God hath made that same Jesus, whom ye have crucified, both Lord and Christ" (v. 36).

It was and is the Holy Ghost who proclaims Him Christ in all men's hearts. He sets the crown upon Him there also, as well as in heaven, so that no man can come to acknowledge Him the Christ except from the Spirit: "No man can say Jesus is the Lord, but by the Holy Ghost" (1 Cor. 12:3). So no matter what right He had in His person or by His Father's designation (Acts 2:36; Rom. 14:9), yet it was the Spirit who publicly proclaimed Him such to all His subjects. To use Christ's own words, He it is that glorifies Me, showing it to them (John 16:14). All this the Holy Spirit has done to and for Christ our Head.

33

Never Leaving Christ Out[1]

"That in the ages to come he might shew the exceeding riches of his grace in his kindness toward us through (or in) Christ Jesus."

—Ephesians 2:7

Why is this phrase "in Christ Jesus," which Paul has used so often before, added again and again?

It is added not just because he would have us never to leave Jesus Christ out. I do not know who can begin without Christ or continue without Christ. I am sure the apostle never leaves him out; no, not in election and adoption, nor in anything, and not now, when he comes to heaven; whatever he speaks of, Christ comes in.

But this is not all; his meaning is that all the glory the saints shall have from those exceeding riches of His grace in heaven shall all be in Christ. He had told them that God had blessed them with all heavenly blessings in Christ (Eph. 1:3–4). If we have heavenly blessings in Christ while upon earth, it will be much more so then; the more heavenly they are, the more they are in Christ. Indeed, outside of Christ God could not love any creature, nor would love any creature, much less would permit any creature to be near

1. From *Ephesians*; *Works* 2:278.

Him, but He has blessed them and will continue to be kind to them in Christ.

In the second place, this phrase is added for a greater, more emphatic purpose, and no greater purpose can be mentioned—to show that all God will bestow on us in heaven shall be out of the same kindness He bears toward Jesus Christ Himself. He will treat you kindly when you come there. Think how kindly He treated His Son, how welcome He made Him when He came to heaven, when He said, "Sit thou here, till I make thine enemies thy footstool" (Ps. 110:1). Why, the same kindness He bears to Christ He bears to us, and out of that kindness He bears to Christ He will entertain us there forevermore, and heartily and freely spend His utmost riches upon us, for He will glorify the Head and the members with the same glory.

Therefore, the apostle showed in the first chapter that He set up Jesus Christ as the Head, and the same power that worked in Him, raised Him up, and set Him in heaven also works in us and shall accomplish it all in us. Here he shows that with the same kindness with which He embraced Jesus Christ as the Head, He embraces the whole body, and out of that kindness He will entertain them everlastingly, as He has done for Jesus Christ. As we and Christ make one body, so God's love to Christ and us is one love. There is one Father, one Spirit, and one love, and indeed one Christ; for both body and Head make one Christ. I need not prove this further, for we see it in John 17:23: "Thou hast loved them, as thou hast loved me." Likewise, verse 22: "The glory which thou gavest me I have given them." What more could be said to show us how great the glory of the riches of His grace in heaven will be? Not only is Jesus Christ a pattern and example of it, but it proceeds out of the same kindness that God has toward Jesus Christ Himself.

John Calvin (1509–1564)

Speaking of Calvin's *Institutes of the Christian Religion*, Goodwin said: "O how sweet was the reading of some parts of that book to me! How pleasing was the delivery of truths in a solid manner to me!"

34

The Mystery of His Will in Christ[1]

"Having made known unto us
the mystery of his will."
— Ephesians 1:9

The will of God is the foundation of the gospel. What will you resolve it into? You must resolve it into His will, and nothing else. "I will have mercy"; this is the gospel, but His will is the foundation of it. "I will have mercy upon whom I will have mercy"; and His will sets His understanding to work, as it were, to find out ways to bring about the salvation of mankind. He works all things after the counsel of His own will, as it follows afterward (Eph. 1:13). Hence, therefore, it is called the mystery of His will.

I will give you another reason for it, which is the better reason for you, because the most comfortable thing we know in the gospel is that it is the will of God to save sinners. Mark what I say—if you knew all that God knows (which is saying something very great) but you did not know that His mind and will were to save sinners, you would be undone; the knowledge of this is worth all the rest. To know that God is merciful in His nature is not enough. You might have known that and despaired, for it might

1. From *Ephesians; Works* 1:142–44.

have been said, "It is true, He is merciful in His nature, but the question is whether He *will* be merciful or not." But He says, "I *will* have mercy"; this word is worth all the world, for this is the gospel.

It is called the mystery of His will because you might have known that Jesus Christ had died, but if you had not known that it was the will of God to accept that death for sinners, you would have been undone still. What does the apostle say in Hebrews 10:10 when he speaks of the influence of the sacrifice of Christ in our salvation? "I came to do thy will," He says. By this will we are sanctified through the offering of the body of Jesus Christ once for all. What saves you? What sanctifies you? It is not simply the offering of the blood of Christ; if you had heard that Christ had died, that would not have comforted you, had it not been for this will. By this will you are sanctified through the offering of the body of Christ.

Let me make two observations from this truth. Observation 1: Do you see, my brethren, the essence of the gospel? It is the mystery of God's will; to know simply that God will save sinners in the blood of Christ is the essence of the gospel. This is that which is essential to salvation. And you see, too, that it is but a small thing to know that God will save sinners in Christ. How gracious God has been! He has not required you to know all the hard things in the gospel—things that scholars know, and many believers who have large understandings—in order to be saved. But this is the kernel of all: God will save sinners. It is the mystery of His will. Do you know this? Has this truth taken hold in your heart?

If you know no more than this, you know that which will save you; you know that which faith may feed upon, that which will make you everlastingly happy. "But," says a poor soul when it begins to believe this in earnest, "will God save sinners, even me? Does God have a mind to save such sinners as I am? I have reason to be content to be saved then." So he gives up his soul to God and to Christ, and the bargain is made. Faith will know the mystery of His will; it is resolved to do so.

I will give you one familiar example of why the knowledge of this one thing is worth all the rest. Suppose that one had lived in Solomon's time, had been a subject to Solomon and a great favorite in his court, but had run into treason, so that it was in Solomon's power to take away his life. But suppose Solomon treated him exceeding kindly and opened to him all his heart. You know that Solomon had the most knowledge that any man ever had, both in matters of nature and in the book of the law. Suppose Solomon should have told all his notions (and he had as many notions in his head as there was sand on the seashore, for he had a vast knowledge) to this poor man, being a traitor and in Solomon's power to put him to death when he would. If he had known but one thing—that Solomon would say to him, "I will pardon your treason, I will save you, you shall not die"—this would have pleased him more than all the knowledge Solomon could have imparted to him. So I say that we are traitors and have deserved death, and it is in God's power to destroy us. If now God reveals to you that His intention is to save sinners, even if He conceals other things from you, even if you do not have a large understanding and cannot take in much, still this you know, that God has a mind to save sinners in Christ, and you can give yourself up to Him. But do you know further that He means to save *you*? It is worth all other knowledge in the world. Why? Because it is the mystery of His will.

Observation 2: See the grace of God in applying Himself to all sorts of believers, in revealing the gospel to weak as well as strong; He has accommodated Himself to weak capacities. If the gospel lay hidden in great wisdom and rationalities, so that a man must know all the depths of wisdom in it, all the rationalities of it, and the coherence of one truth with another before he could be saved, many poor, weak understandings would have despaired and never should have come to be saved. But God loads your hearts with only one truth—He will save sinners *in* and *through* Christ. Have you learned this in the gospel? This will save you; the gospel is the mystery of His will.

And, my brethren, He has accommodated Himself to weak understandings in faith, too. Why did He choose faith of all graces by which to save a man? Because the poorest and weakest understanding in the world can believe and trust. When he hears that God saves sinners, he is able to trust God as strongly and as firmly as the wisest man in the world. Nay, weak men are most apt to believe; they are more suited for faith. Let them simply have this revealed to them, that God will save poor sinners; salvation lies in trust. When a man's heart is convinced of this—and a poor soul is able to do it—he does it as strongly as the greatest understanding in the world can do it.

35

Treasures in Heaven[1]

Adam in his best condition was merely flesh and blood, an earthly man, as he is termed in distinction from Christ (1 Cor. 15:47). And as that earthly man was, such we should have been, since we are of him who was of earthly generation, and neither he nor we would have advanced higher (v. 48). But our Lord Christ is the Lord from heaven, a heavenly man (vv. 47–48). Therefore, as we are blessed in and together with Him, we are blessed in heavenly things or with heavenly blessings, and raised up to heavenly places with Him. Because Christ is the heavenly man, such is the condition of those in Him; we are heavenly as He Himself is. Heaven is His native country and He is the Lord of it. Since we are married to Him and He is our Lord in that respect, and since, as was said, the spouse must be where the husband is and partake of the same good things of which he partakes, therefore Christ takes us and carries us to His own home, to His Father's house, which is heaven. We thereby come to be blessed in Christ with all heavenly blessings, not spiritual blessings only, with which Adam in his primitive condition was blessed.

All the graces we have are not only spiritual, to fit us for communion with God on earth, but they are

1. From *Ephesians*; *Works* 1:57–58.

preparations that make us more fit for the inheritance in light, to see God face to face. They all tend to lead us in the way to heaven and to bring us to heaven at last, and they have all the promises of heavenly things annexed to and entailed upon them.

"Follow me, and you shall have treasure in heaven," says Christ; we shall have a more enduring substance in the heavens, as Paul speaks (Heb. 10:34). All things that are in heaven and are found growing there are ours, and we have an interest in them, just as those in Canaan had to all the earthly things that country afforded and abounded with. For the enjoyment of the things in that world, at the resurrection our bodies will be made spiritual and heavenly, which Adam's was not. Our bodies will be raised as spiritual bodies (1 Cor. 15). There is a spiritual body, that which is received at the resurrection, and there is a natural body, that in which Adam was created (v. 44). So it is written, "The first Adam was made a living soul, an earthly man" (v. 45), but Christ and His saints are made spiritual, heavenly, so that in verse 48 he evidently applies this to the state of the body.

That natural body of Adam was framed with such inlets and capacities of outward senses as were suited to take in all the good things that God had made and provided in this world on purpose for him—meats for the belly and the belly for meats (1 Cor. 6:13). Just as on earth there is a plurality and a variety of things, so it is in heaven, and so that we may be capable of taking similar comfort from these heavenly things (which are far more transcendent in goodness, so as to afford greater goodness to us), our very bodies shall be fitted and suited thereunto, being made heavenly and spiritual, with inlets and capacities heavenly and spiritual. Our bodies shall be made capable of pleasure in the created excellencies there, in the framing or contriving of which God has showed so much of His art and skill. In particular, our bodies will receive a glory and happiness in and from the presence of that heavenly body of Christ, our bodies and His being suited to each other in a heavenly manner and way. The words of 1 Corinthians 6:13–14 insinuate this clearly. And if our bodies are so transformed, to what heavenly state and glorious capacity shall the soul be raised, to take in those pleasures that flow immediately from the face of God and the Godhead, whose fullness dwells in that human nature, the body and soul of Christ, in whose presence are rivers of pleasure for evermore!

So God has blessed us with all in heaven, both places and things, to be enjoyed hereafter. In the meantime, He has furnished us with graces and dispositions that in themselves are heavenly and of a higher strain than Adam's, though his were spiritual. God has endued these graces with a right to all those things to be enjoyed in heaven and has entailed all upon them. In the end, He will bring us there and render us fit for the enjoyment of them.

Alexander Whyte (1836–1921)

Scottish Minister at Free St. George's Church in Edinburgh. Whyte wrote a couple of tributes on Goodwin and was deeply influenced by his writings. Concerning Goodwin, Whyte said, "I have read no other author so much and so often. And I continue to read him to this day, as if I had never read him before."

Reading Goodwin

The first collection of Goodwin's works was published in five folio volumes in London from 1681 to 1704, under the editorship of Thankful Owen, Thomas Baron, and Thomas Goodwin Jr. An abridged version of those works was later printed in four volumes (London, 1847–1850). The best-known and definitive twelve-volume edition was printed by James Nichol (Edinburgh, 1861–1866) in the Nichol's Series of Standard Divines, then reissued in 1996 by Tanski Publications and in 2006 by Reformation Heritage Books.

Goodwin's exegesis is massive; he leaves no stone unturned. His first editors (1681) said of his work: "He had a genius to dive into the bottom of points, to 'study them down,' as he used to express it, not contenting himself with superficial knowledge, without wading into the depths of things."[1] Edmund Calamy put it this way: "It is evident from his writings, he studied not words, but things. His style is plain and familiar; but very diffuse, homely and tedious."[2] One does need patience to read Goodwin at times; however, along with depth and prolixity, he offers a wonderful sense of warmth, piety, and experience. A reader's patience will be amply rewarded.

---

1. See *Works,* 1:xxix–xxxii.

2. Calamy, *Nonconformist's Memorial,* 1:186.

How should a beginner proceed in reading Goodwin's works? Here is a suggested plan (parenthetical notes refer to Nichol's edition of Goodwin's *Works*):

1. Begin by reading some of Goodwin's shorter, more practical writings, such as *Patience and Its Perfect Work*, which includes four sermons on James 1:1–5. This was written after much of Goodwin's personal library was destroyed by fire (2:429–67). It contains much practical instruction on enhancing a spirit of submission.

2. Read *Certain Select Cases Resolved*, which offers three experimental treatises. They reveal Goodwin's pastoral heart for afflicted Christians. Each addresses specific struggles in the believer's soul: (a) "A Child of Light Walking in Darkness" is a classic work of encouragement for the spiritually depressed based on Isaiah 50:10–11 (3:231–350). The subtitle summarizes its contents: "A Treatise shewing The Causes by which, The Cases wherein, and the Ends for which, God leaves His Children to Distress of Conscience, Together with Directions How to Walk so as to Come Forth of Such a Condition." (b) "The Return of Prayers," based on Psalm 85:8, is a uniquely practical work. It offers help in ascertaining "God's answers to our prayers" (3:353–429). (c) "The Trial of a Christian's Growth" (3:433–506), based on John 15:1–2, is a masterpiece on sanctification. It focuses on mortification and vivification. For a mini-classic on spiritual growth, this gem remains unsurpassed.

You might also read *The Vanity of Thoughts*, based on Jeremiah 4:14 (3:509–528). This work, often republished in paperback, stresses the need for bringing every thought captive to Christ. It also describes ways to foster that obedience.

3. Read some of Goodwin's great sermons. Inevitably, they are strong, biblical, Christological, and experimental (2:359–425; 4:151–224; 5:439–548; 7:473–576; 9:499–514; 12:1–127).

4. Delve into Goodwin's works that explain major doctrines, such as:

- *An Unregenerate Man's Guiltiness Before God in Respect of Sin and Punishment* (10:1–567). This is a weighty treatise on human guilt, corruption, and the imputation and punishment of sin. In exposing the total depravity of the natural man's heart, this book is unparalleled. Its aim is to produce a heartfelt need for saving faith in Christ rather than offer the quick fix of superficial Christianity.
- *The Object and Acts of Justifying Faith* (8:1–593). This is a frequently reprinted classic on faith. Part 1, on the *objects of faith*, focuses on God's nature, Christ, and the free grace of God revealed in His absolute promises. Part 2 deals with the *acts of faith*—what it means to believe in Christ, to obtain assurance, to find joy in the Holy Ghost, and to make use of God's electing love. One section beautifully explains the "actings of faith in prayer." Part 3 addresses the *properties of faith*—its excellence in giving all honor to God and Christ; its difficulty in reaching beyond the natural abilities of man; and its necessity in requiring us to believe in the strength of God.

The conclusion provides "directions to guide us in our endeavours to believe."

- *Christ the Mediator* (2 Cor. 5:18–19), *Christ Set Forth* (Rom. 8:34), and *The Heart of Christ in Heaven Towards Sinners on Earth* are great works on Christology (5:1–438; 4:1–92; 4:93–150). *Christ the Mediator* sets forth Jesus in His substitutionary work of humiliation. It rightly deserves to be called a classic. *Christ Set Forth* proclaims Christ in His exaltation, and *The Heart of Christ* explores the tenderness of Christ's glorified human nature shown to His people on earth. Goodwin is more mystical in this latter work than anywhere else in his writings, but as Paul Cook has ably shown, his mysticism is kept within the boundaries of Scripture.[3] Whyte says Goodwin is unparalleled "in his combination of intellectual and theological power with evangelical and homiletical comfort."[4] This particular work of Goodwin's may be his most impressive in terms of combining rich Christology with warm practical piety.

- *Gospel Holiness in Heart and Life* (7:129–336) is a convicting masterpiece based on Philippians 1:9–11. It explains the doctrine of sanctification in every sphere of life.

- *The Knowledge of God the Father, and His Son Jesus Christ* (4:347–569), combined with *The*

---

3. Paul Cook, "Thomas Goodwin—Mystic?" in *Diversities of Gifts,* 45–56.

4. Whyte, *Thirteen Appreciations,* 165.

Work of the Holy Spirit (6:1–522), explores the profound work in the believer's soul of each of the three divine persons. *The Work of the Holy Spirit* is particularly helpful for understanding the doctrines of regeneration and conversion. It carefully distinguishes the work of "the natural conscience" from the Spirit's saving work.

- *The Glory of the Gospel* (4:227–346) consists of two sermons and a treatise based on Colossians 1:26–27. It should be read along with *The Blessed State of Glory Which the Saints Possess After Death* (7:339–472), based on Revelation 14:13.
- *A Discourse of Election* (9:1–498) delves deeply into issues such as the supralapsarian–infralapsarian debate, which wrestles with the moral or rational order of God's decrees. It also deals with the practical fruits of election (e.g., see Book IV on 1 Peter 5:10 and Book V on how God fulfills His covenant of grace in the generations of believers).
- *The Creatures and the Condition of Their State by Creation* (7:1–128). Goodwin is more philosophical in this work than in others.

5. Prayerfully and slowly digest Goodwin's 900-plus-page exposition of Ephesians 1:1 to 2:11 (1:1–564; 2:1–355). Whyte wrote of this work, "Not even Luther on the Galatians is such an expositor of Paul's mind and heart as is Goodwin on the Ephesians."[5]

5. Ibid., 162.

6. Save for last Goodwin's exposition of Revelation (3:1–226) and his only polemical work, *The Constitution, Right Order, and Government of the Churches of Christ* (11:1–546). Independents would highly value this polemic, while Presbyterians probably wouldn't, saying Goodwin is trustworthy on every subject except church government. Goodwin's work does not degrade Presbyterians, however. One of his contemporaries, who argued against Goodwin's view on church government, confessed that Goodwin conveyed "a truly great and noble spirit" throughout the work.[6]

6. Ibid., 169.